GDPR - Fix it Fast

APPLY GDPR TO YOUR COMPANY IN 10 SIMPLE STEPS

Patrick O'Kane

Brentham House Publishing Company

Covent Garden

GDPR - FIX IT FAST, APPLY GDPR TO YOUR COMPANY IN 10 SIMPLE STEPS

@2017 by Patrick O'Kane. All rights reserved.

Brentham House Publishing Company
71-75 Shelton Street
Covent Garden
London, WC2H 9JQ

Brentham House Publishing Company books may be purchased for educational, business or sales promotional use. For information, please email the Special Markets Department at Info@BrenthamHousePublishing.com.

FIRST EDITION

A CIP Record of this book is available from the British Library

ISBN: 978-0-9934788-5-7 (soft cover edition)

ISBN: 978-0-9934788-6-4 (electronic edition)

Brentham House
Publishing Company Ltd.
COVENT GARDEN

Table of Contents

Introduction...1

Step 1: Appointing Royalty: The Data Protection Officer 11

Step 2: Complete the Data Audit – Otherwise Known As: Where is All Your Data? 17

Step 3: Make Your Data Map 29

Step 4: Get Straight on Security 37

Step 5: Tell it Like it Is with Privacy Notices...51

Step 6: Get it in Writing – Staff Policies..61

Step 7: Get on the Training Train 69

Step 8: Measuring the Impact with PIAs 77

Step 9: What to Do When It All Goes Wrong: Preparing for and Reporting Data Breaches 87

Step 10: Dealing with Third-Party Pain...101

What Now? Record, Record, Record...107

Putting it All Together..115

Index...125

Table of Contents

To my parents, John and Roisin O'Kane

Foreword

"WHAT DO YOU MEAN I can't export the email immediately to the United States? It's the company's email. It's not like I'm asking for their personal Gmail. Why can't we have it?" I protested. I was in my second year of practicing law at a major Los Angeles-based law firm. Our firm's London office been asked to perform a large internal investigation for a Swiss bank that had offices all over the world. I immediately requested the corporate emails of the target but was told I couldn't have them. Why? Data privacy and Swiss banking secrecy law.

I was baffled. Data privacy? I thought that only referred to data breaches where financial records were concerned. I'd received a couple of notifications that my credit card numbers had been compromised over the years, but I'd never heard of corporate email being owned by the employee.

In 2011, I moved to London to work on the case. Data privacy issues quickly became a constant consideration for me, and I took it on with gusto. Soon I was drafting articles in Compliance and Ethics Professional Magazine and The Lawyer about data privacy issues. I was fascinated and made it my mission to translate data privacy considerations to Americans who were unfamiliar with them, and to explain to Europeans why Americans had never come across these concerns.

Fast forward to April 2016, when GDPR was adopted (it was fully implemented and enforceable from 25 May 2018). Companies scrambled to figure out how to apply this law to their current practices. They grappled with the extra-territorial reach. American companies selling to Europeans suddenly had to understand consent, the role of data processors and data controllers, and the right to be forgotten. For many, it seemed a daunting task.

GDPR's penalties strike fear in the heart of executives and boards. Data privacy practitioners, compliance offers, information technology, and security folks have been tasked with GDPR implementation, often without a road map or assistance.

That's why Patrick wrote this book. It's a clear, concise text that breaks down GDPR implementation into 10 simple steps. As I read through the draft of the book, I was struck by how readable it was. It's full of examples and exercises to help anyone tasked with GDPR implementation to complete their duty without angst and tears.

If you're an American newbie who has been asked to implement policies and procedures so your company can comply with GDPR – welcome. If you're a long-time European data practitioner –

welcome to you, too. The explanations and exercises in this book will ensure that you've got a solid road map and a plan to complete your implementation flawlessly.

As Patrick says in the book, GDPR implementation can be made simple, but the execution is sometimes hard. If you've been looking for help in plain English, this book is for you. Moving from fear to action can be difficult, but with Patrick and his roadmap by your side, you too can be successful in implementing GDPR.

\-   Kristy Grant-Hart

CEO, Spark Compliance Consulting Ltd. and author of How to Be a Wildly Effective Compliance Officer and the Wildly STRATEGIC Compliance Officer Workbook.

Introduction

CAST YOUR MIND BACK to the first time you used the Internet. Perhaps it was in an Internet café, in a library, or at a friend's house. The sound of a dial tone and a number being dialed. The whistles and beeps followed by the low, interminable hiss of a connection being made. It was the sound of the rising Internet. The sound of progress.

These were more innocent days, when personal data was usually held in filing cabinets and when data transfers took place by post. The most advanced companies held data on floppy disks. This was when the interconnected world of today was barely envisioned, even by the most prophetic.

Twenty years later, and after much lobbying by business and arguing by governments, the new tablets have come down from the mountain. I refer, of course, to the new European General Data Protection Regulation (which I refer to as "GDPR" going forward). In these 88 pages lies the future. A law that affects companies around the world selling to customers in the EU. A world in which governments with lax privacy laws can't give get-out-of-jail-free cards to companies serving the European population. The interconnected, data-driven, big data world has arrived. The Wild West era is over, and the new regulation will crack down hard on companies that play fast and loose with customer data.

It won't be easy. Many approach the law with fear and apprehension. Its complexities loom large, with massive fines as penalties for inaction. Information Security, Information Technology, Legal, and Compliance personnel must work together to comply. The magnitude of the changes is keeping executives up at night.

But although GDPR is a challenging regulation, you can turn it to your advantage if you approach it in the correct way.

My Data Story

I qualified as a lawyer in 2000, the year Y2K didn't arrive. It was also the year that led to one of the landmark privacy cases in the UK. It involved Michael Douglas and Catherine Zeta-Jones. The case concerned their right to privacy in relation to unauthorized publication of photographs of their wedding.

I first worked in private practice and many of my cases had a privacy element relating to the UK Human Rights Act. I advised many citizens about their privacy rights and acted for a vast array of clients from ordinary workers to criminal defendants. Everyone enjoys some expectation of privacy. Working in and out of different courts, I learned how strange and engaging privacy law can be.

I grew up in a family of brothers, so I always loved debate. When I was older, I loved that there was so much debate around privacy law. How much privacy could one expect? And what competing interests must we consider when we think about privacy? How far could one go in sacrificing privacy? What sacrifices should be made, for example, to prevent crime? All these things drew me to privacy law.

Later, I became a Qualified Data Protection Practitioner and have worked as an in-house lawyer and Data Protection Officer. I worked for an excellent and innovative group of companies with offices throughout the UK and Europe called Markerstudy. Markerstudy has a presence in a number of sectors including insurance and aviation. They take compliance and data protection very seriously.

I was lucky to lead the GDPR compliance project for Markerstudy. I gained great experience in running such a large-scale GDPR compliance project.

In putting GDPR into practice, I have worked with hundreds of employees across various departments including Marketing, Information Technology, Security, Legal, and Human Resources. This experience was invaluable for me in learning what does and does not work when completing GDPR implementation. I want to show you what works and help you avoid wasting time. I will help you to avoid inefficient use of resources.

As the Data Protection Officer for Markerstudy, I found myself wanting help. While there were many academic guides debating the nuances of the different Articles of GDPR, there weren't any truly practical guides that spoke in plain English about what needs to be done. I wanted to create a clear, straightforward guidebook that would lead data practitioners through the GDPR evaluation, planning, and implementation process in an understandable way.

There were some big challenges. How do you make sure hundreds of thousands of customers are getting the correct privacy information? How do you run a large project across many departments and make sure everyone is doing what they are supposed to do? What parts of GDPR are the priorities for the company, and which parts can we ignore? Who makes the big decisions when a company reaches a fork in the road during a part of the project? I faced all of these challenges and many more, and I want to use my experience to help you understand the best way forward for your own GDPR implementation.

What this book will do for you

This book lays out 10 simple steps to GDPR compliance. While the steps may be simple to explain, they can be complex in practice. This has led to fear and inaction in many companies. Like it or not, the GDPR is here, so practitioners must move from fear and into action. Consider this book your guidebook – your road map to compliance.

Throughout the book you'll find examples, checklists and exercises to help you implement your privacy program in a GDPR-compliant way. By the time you finish this book, you will have a cohesive, comprehensive plan you can implement quickly and efficiently.

GDPR – What is the point?

The last time there was a major change to EU data privacy laws, back in 1995, 0.4% of the world's population used the Internet. Now more than 50% of people across the globe are online.[1]

In the Internet age, companies process more personal data (which we'll shorten to "data" in this book, as we're only talking about personal data) than ever before. This includes everything from browsing history to credit history. GDPR puts stringent rules on the increasingly sophisticated data processing that companies are carrying out across the globe.

I have summarized the main changes that GDPR makes to the Regulatory landscape below. These aren't all the changes, but they're the main ones you should be aware of before we start on the ten steps. This is not an academic book, so you will need to go to other resources for the full detail of GDPR.

Who does it apply to? Article 3

The GDPR applies to both Data Processors and Data Controllers, although it applies to them in different ways. More on this later.

Where does it apply? Article 3

It applies to companies processing personal data:

- If they are established in the EU, even if the data processing takes place outside the EU
- If they are not established in the EU but the data processing relates to:
    o offering goods or services to people in the EU
    o monitoring the behavior of people in the EU.

For example, a U.S. company that offers its watches for sale in the EU is subject to GDPR.

Under GDPR, companies based outside the EU that are caught by the regulation will have to appoint a representative within the EU to make sure customers have a contact point for concerns relating to their data. They must also tell the Supervisory Authority/Regulator who their representative is.

GDPR applies to all data subjects about whom you hold data, including employees and contractors, but I will refer to "customers" throughout the text for ease of reference.

Data Processors – Article 4

A Data Processor is someone who carries out data processing on the Controller's behalf. GDPR applies to both Controllers and Processors (see Article 3). Controllers will bear ultimate responsibility for the data processing under GDPR but Processors are much more "in the frame" now than they were under the previous EU law and are subject to much of GDPR. Processors must retain records and have more liability if they cause a data breach.

If you are a Processor (processing the data of EU customers on behalf of a Controller) and you are:

- Established in the EU, then GDPR applies to you, even if the processing takes place outside the EU
- Not established in the EU but your data processing is related to offering goods and services to customers in the EU, then GDPR applies to you
- Not established in the EU but your data processing is related to monitoring the behaviour of customers in the EU, then GDPR applies to you

An example of a Processor is a cloud service provider or a company that provides your company with call center services. Processors do not have the right to make any decisions over the data. They are merely servants of Controller.

Processors have new responsibilities under GDPR and they can be hit with fines for breaches of GDPR.

Processors must also make sure they keep adequate records of any processing they carry out and must process the data securely. Most of the 10 Simple Steps will apply to Controllers and Processors, although Processors are not under the same obligations to issue Privacy Notices to customers, nor are they under the same obligations to implement a Privacy Impact Assessment process.

Huge penalties – Article 83

There are two tiers of penalties under GDPR, both of which can be found under Article 83.

The maximum fine for breach of GDPR is 4% of global annual turnover or €20 million (whichever is higher). These fines will usually relate to a breach of a data subject's rights or any of the basic GDPR principles.

There is a lower tier of fines of 2% of global annual turnover or €10 million (whichever is higher) for administrative breaches, such as failing to appoint a Data Protection Officer, failing to report a data breach when required to do so, or breaching the rules on consent.

Regulators do not have carte blanche to fine as much as they want for any GDPR breach. Article 83 of GDPR says the fines must be "proportionate" to the GDPR breach. I strongly suspect that major fines will be reserved for major data breaches.

Data rights Articles 12-23

GDPR focuses heavily on giving individuals more control over their data. There are numerous rights set out from Articles 12-23 of GDPR.

Some of the more important changes to customer rights are detailed below.

Data Portability – Article 20

The right to data portability is an entirely new right. It means customers have a right to demand you collect all of the data you hold on them and to transfer it over to a new provider. A company must comply with such a request within one month (usually) and must provide the transfer free of charge. The customer only has this right where it is technically feasible for the company to transfer the data.

The right to data portability is a restricted right and only applies:

- to personal data a customer has provided to a controller;
- where the processing is based on the customer's consent or for the performance of a contract

Let's say, for example, that Kate has been banking with one bank for 10 years. She's decided to change to a new bank and wants to take all of her financial records with her. The right to data portability allows Kate to ask her old bank to transfer all of her data to her new bank in "a structured, commonly used and machine-readable form" This means the old bank must transfer the records in a way that is easy for the new bank to use.

Kate's old bank should make sure they have proper procedures in place to comply with the right to date portability, and should have some template letters of response to customers who contact them looking to exercise the right.

Right to Erasure – Article 17

The right to erasure allows the customer to wipe his data off your systems and to make sure that any third-party with which you have shared the data does so also. This is a major overhaul of an existing right.

The right to erasure is not an absolute right. There are a number of restrictions. For instance, a company may retain customer data in anticipation of a legal claim and the company may keep certain data in order to comply with legal obligations.

Let's say Megan booked a hotel for her wedding reception. Megan was very unhappy with the service on her big day, and most of the wedding party complained about the food. Megan was upset and has threatened to sue the hotel. She demands the hotel immediately wipe her data from their systems. There is a strong reason here for the hotel to retain some of the Megan's data because they anticipate that she may take legal action.

In the instances where Customer X successfully exercises his right to erasure, you will have to delete his data off your systems and make sure any third parties that are holding Customer X's data on your behalf delete it also (unless it is a disproportionate effort to do so).

Companies will have to make sure they have new procedures and policies in place so their employees know how to handle these requests correctly. The company should also have a bank of template letters of response in place for customers who want to exercise the right.

Right of access – Article 15

The right of access gives individuals the ability to access the personal data a company holds about them. To exercise this right, individuals must serve the company with a Subject Access Request. Companies have one month within which to comply with a Subject Access Request under GDPR. Companies can no longer charge a fee to a customer that wishes to enforce the right.

You may have to change your company's existing procedures to reflect the new rules around Subject Access Requests. The right of access is a huge part of data compliance. In fact, in the UK, there are more complaints in relation to right of access requests from data subjects than any other issue.

Employees of companies are data subjects, and they enjoy all these rights against their employer.

Data Breach Notification – Article 33

Companies have new responsibilities to report certain data breaches to the Regulator and to customers. Processors have responsibilities here too, as they must tell Controllers about breaches without undue delay. (see Step 9: What to do if it all Goes Wrong - Data Breach Reporting).

Data Protection Officers – Article 37

In certain cases, companies will have a legal requirement to appoint a suitably qualified Data Protection Officer. This applies whether the company is a Controller or a Processor. (More on this can be found in Step 1: Anointing Data Royalty - the Data Protection Officer).

Automated Decision Making – Article 22

There are strict rules around getting a computer to make a decision about a customer if the decision has a significant or legal effect on the customer. This includes 'profiling', i.e. analyzing a customer's behavior or characteristics by computer.

Risk Assessments – Article 35

Under Articles 35 and 36 of GDPR, controllers have to carry out an assessment of the privacy risk for new projects if the project uses new technology and it is likely to result in a high risk to the rights and freedoms of customers.

Carrying out a risk assessment means that the company should complete a Privacy Impact Assessment ("PIA") form before embarking on a new project. (See Step 7: Assessing the Impact with PIAs).

For instance, if a music app wants to profile all their customers in Belgium to see whether sales increase if these customers receive pop-up ads of the latest song releases, then a PIA should be completed before this goes ahead.

Another example might occur if a handbag company is launching an expensive new design. If the company decides to send marketing emails to all customers who have made a purchase of more than $500 on a single handbag last year, a PIA should be completed before this goes ahead if it meets the criteria for PIAs as set out in Article 35 and 36.

Records – Article 5

Under Article 5(2), Controllers must be able to "demonstrate compliance" under GDPR.
This means you must be able to "show not tell" the Regulator how you are complying with GDPR.
One aspect of showing compliance is keeping proper records of data processing.
Examples of records you should keep include:

- Customer consent forms
- Confirmation that data was deleted or corrected
- PIA forms
- Company policies such as your Data Protection Policy and your IT Security Policy
- Records of things you decided not to do – such as deciding not to appoint a Data Protection Officer
- Records of steps you took to mitigate a data breach.

(See What Now? Record, Record, Record for more details).

Pseudonymisation and Anonymization – Article 4

GDPR talks about "pseudonymisation" in Article 4(5). Pseudonymisation is the separation of data from personal identifiers, making a link to the data to a person impossible without additional information, which is held separately. It means all the personal identifiers in the data have been stripped out. In some circumstances, this may be advisable. For example, pseudonymisation may result in your data being held more securely.

Anonymized data is data rendered anonymous in such a way that the data subject is not or is no longer identifiable (Recital 26 of GDPR).

Consent

Often companies rely on customer consent to process their data. If you are relying on consent, there is now a higher standard for consent to be considered valid.

Consent has to be "freely given, specific, informed, and unambiguous."

This means:

- Companies cannot force their customers to hand over consent – For example, you cannot refuse to let a customer enter a competition if he doesn't give you his consent.
- You cannot hide consent language in the small print – For example, let's say David enters a competition with DreamHoliday to win a holiday in Barbados. If DreamHoliday wants to send David marketing emails, they should ask David to check a box saying he is ok to receive marketing.
- Opt-outs are out – Opt-outs exist when the company has pre-checked the box on behalf of the customer. The customer is required to un-check the box if she does not agree with the statement such as:
  - *"I agree for my data to be sold to our trusted business partners who may use it to analyze my purchase history ☑"*

Pre-checked boxes do not qualify as consent under GDPR. For a consent to be valid a customer must DO SOMETHING such as check a box or sign a form himself without these things having already been done for him.

Companies must give the customer a clear way to withdraw consent – Your company must give customers an easy way to contact you to withdraw consent.

For example, if last month Angelina checked a box saying she consented to a company processing her medical data, she may change her mind. Let's say the company has an email address for customers to contact if they withdraw consent. This allows Angelina to email the company to tell them that she has changed her mind about the consent she gave last month. It is important the company then stops processing Angelina's medical data.

Lawfulness of processing conditions

Under GDPR, the conditions for lawful processing of data remain similar to the current law. Basically, you need a valid reason before you can process someone's data. These valid reasons are frequently referred to as "lawful basis" or "conditions for lawful processing." Before you can process a person's data, you must make sure one of the lawfulness of processing conditions applies to you. For personal data, the lawful processing conditions are:

- Consent of the data subject
- Processing is necessary for the performance of a contract with the data subject
- Processing is necessary for compliance with a legal obligation
- Processing is necessary to protect the vital interests of a data subject or another person
- Processing is necessary for the performance of a task carried out in the public interest or in the exercise of official authority vested in the controller

- Processing is necessary for the purposes of legitimate interests pursued by the controller or a third party, except where such interests are overridden by the interests, rights, or freedoms of the data subject

There are further conditions for special categories of data. Please see the full text of GDPR for more details.

This Isn't the Whole Story

There are many aspects of GDPR that may need to be considered by your company. These may include changes related to data transfers, processing principles, definitions, and rights that are part of GDPR and represent less fundamental changes to existing law. There are, of course, many terms that remain similar to the pre-GDPR law, so please check to see how the laws apply to your company. You should also look to see which aspects of GDPR affect you if you are a Processor rather than a Controller.

Now that we've got the basic changes down, let's move ahead to put the new rules into practice in your company. To do this, we're going to follow the 10 simple steps that will move you from fear to action.

Ten Simple Steps

Our ten-step process goes like this:

Step 1: Appointing Royalty: The Data Protection Officer
Step 2: Complete the Data Audit - Otherwise Known As - Where Is All Your Data?
Step 3: Make Your Data Map
Step 4: Get Straight on Security
Step 5: Tell it like it is with Privacy Notices
Step 6: Get it in Writing: Privacy Policies
Step 7: Get on the Training Train
Step 8: Assessing the Impact with PIAs
Step 9: What to do if it All Goes Wrong - Data Breach Reporting
Step 10: Dealing with Third Party Pain

By following our ten-step plan, you'll be on the road to compliance in no time.

Which Step do I take first?

Steps 1, 2 and 3 must be done first. Steps 4 through 10 do not need to be done in sequence. You may find that you are tackling some of Steps 4 to 10 concurrently. It is best to read the entire book so you have a better idea of the priority of the remaining steps. It may seem overwhelming at first, but we will take it one step at a time. Speaking of, let's get on with Step 1 – anointing data royalty – the Data Protection Officer.

Notes on Implementation

_____

_____

_____

_____

_____

_____

_____

_____

_____

_____

_____

_____

_____

_____

_____

_____

STEP 1

Appointing Royalty:
The Data Protection Officer

EVERY GREAT STORY NEEDS a hero, and in our quest for data protection mastery, one figure emerges from the fog to lead the company toward the light: the Data Protection Officer (DPO). Part guardian, part guide, this role is filled with peril. For those brave enough to choose the mantle of "DPO," great treasures await. But first, they must conquer GDPR.

When do you have to appoint a Data Protection Officer?

Not every organization is required to have a Data Protection Officer (DPO). In small companies where there is little data processing, it wouldn't make sense to have one. However, under Article 37 of GDPR, your company must appoint a DPO if:

- You are a public body; or
- You carry out monitoring of individuals on a large scale (for example you monitor people's online behaviour); or
- Your "core activities" consist of large scale processing of special categories of data (special categories include data about race, religion, health, sex life, and sexual orientation) or criminal data (which for some strange reason is not a special category of data).

If you fail to appoint a DPO when you should, you could be in line for a large fine of up to 2% of global annual turnover or €10 million.

Do Processors have to appoint DPOs?

If your company falls into any of the categories above, it must appoint a DPO. It must do so whether it is a Processor or a Controller.

For example, let's say UltraStorage is a cloud storage provider. Their business is entirely in the United States, but they've been hired by Golden Futures, a UK health insurance company, to store all of their customer's health data. Golden Futures has 1 million customers. Even though UltraStorage is only a Processor under GDPR (i.e. they have to do what they are told with the data) they still must appoint a DPO, because they are processing health data, which is a special category of data.

Can I appoint a DPO for a Group of companies?

Yes, you can appoint a DPO for a Group of companies. A single DPO may cover a Group as long as the DPO is given enough resource to do the job.

What if I am not obliged to appoint a DPO under GDPR? Can I appoint one anyway?

You can appoint a DPO voluntarily even if you aren't legally required. If you appoint a DPO when you are not legally required to do so, you must follow all of the GDPR relating to DPOs. The DPO must:

- Report to the highest level of authority in the company
- Not have any conflicts of interest in performing his/her role
- Have the support of senior management

Why would I appoint a DPO if I don't have to?

A DPO can help keep you on the right side of law by putting the correct procedures in place to make sure data is used in the right way. She can train staff and warn the company if it goes down the wrong path. So if the DPO is doing her job properly, she has the potential to prevent the company from getting into trouble with the Regulator and perhaps even avoid fines.

The downside to appointing a DPO when you are not legally required to do so you is that you will still be caught by all the rules of Article 37. Appointing a DPO when you do not have to might seem like a great idea, but you should be aware that you will be subject to more rules and responsibilities.

What's in a name?

A Company that does not legally have to appoint a DPO may want to hire a data protection expert to keep it on the right side of GDPR. One solution may be to appoint a data protection expert but to call them something different from "Data Protection Officer." For example, you could call the person a "Privacy Manager" or a "Privacy Advisor" or something of that nature. It is not yet 100% clear whether having a DPO by another name would take you outside the scope of the duties on companies under Article 37. If you have to appoint a DPO under GDPR, the person must be given the title of Data Protection Officer.

Can the DPO have other jobs in the company or is he only allowed to be DPO?

Yes. The DPO can have other jobs in the company as long as they do not interfere with her duties as DPO.

For smaller companies or those not processing a lot of data, the DPO job may only be part of an employee's duties. If a company appoints a DPO, it must ensure there is no conflict of interest between the DPO's duties and any other duties they may have.

For example, if the DPO of a small company was also on the sales team there could be a conflict of interest. This is because she might be under pressure to send marketing emails to clients to encourage sales, which might hamper her ability to give objective advice as DPO.

What is the DPO supposed to do?

Under GDPR, the DPO should have adequate experience and knowledge of data protection law and practices. The DPO has a number of tasks set down in GDPR including:

- Advising the company on GDPR and data protection laws
- Monitoring GDPR compliance
- Providing advice on data protection Risk Assessments (more on this in step 4)
- Dealing with Regulators
- Being a contact point on all things data protection
- Manage data processing risks

What else do companies have to do when they appoint a DPO?

Under Article 38 of GDPR there are a few more responsibilities for companies:

- The DPO must be involved in all data protection issues – the company can't keep the DPO in the dark about any privacy issues that are happening in the company.
- The DPO must have enough support and resources from the company do his job properly
- The DPO must operate independently of the rest of the business and cannot be fired for carrying out her tasks. To do so is a breach of GDPR.
- The DPO "shall directly report to the highest management level" of the company. What does this mean? Like so much of GDPR this is open to interpretation. My opinion is that the DPO should regularly report to the Board of Directors either in-person or in written reports. The point of this part of Article 38 is to ensure that the DPO has a "red telephone" that goes straight to the powers that be to warn the company if they are getting into hot water with their data processing.
- Customers and other data subjects can contact the DPO with questions relating to their data.

The company can't keep the DPO in the dark about any privacy issues that are happening in the company.

What are the benefits of being a DPO?

The first major benefit of being a DPO is that it becomes extremely difficult to fire you. The company cannot fire you for voicing your opinion on their data processing activities, as you are required to be independent by law. Job security is a nice benefit of the DPO role.

Another benefit of the role is the ability to report directly to the Board or the CEO. Depending on where you are now in the hierarchy, this could be a big boost in your visibility at the company.

DPOs take on tremendous responsibility. When the DPO role is done effectively, you become a strategic partner to the business. You can be helpful in setting the stage for the company's growth and innovation in the digital marketplace. In short, the DPO can be a cool new role that's challenging and fun.

What are the downsides to being a DPO?

With great power comes great responsibility. The DPO's job is to stand up to the business when the business wants to process data in a way that is contrary to the law. When a law is principles-based, such as is the case with the GDPR, some activities fall into a grey area. Is the activity strictly allowed or disallowed? If the answer is "maybe," the DPO may have to make very unpopular decisions.

If the company is aggressively pursuing marketing strategies and big data analytics that will make-or-break profitability, it is easy for the DPO to feel marginalized if her advice is not respected. If the company ends up with fines and reputational damage based on its processing activities, the DPO may find it difficult to get another job, even if the she spoke out against the activities.

The DPO cannot be a shrinking violet. She must be able to stand up to people in the organization and tell them when they are violating GDPR. This does not mean she has to shout and slam doors, but it does mean that she will have to disagree with some high-profile people in his company.

The Big 3 – The Cost-Saving Advantages of Having a DPO

1. **Saving company time** – Often when a data query comes in and there is no assigned DPO, the query can bounce around the Legal and Compliance Department while people try to figure out what to do with it. When the query is finally assigned to someone, they spend valuable company hours scratching their heads and wondering what to do next. Having a DPO in place means that all of these data queries can be dealt with efficiently and in the correct way, which can lead to saving resources over the long term.

2. **The fines that will never be** – From big data analytics to targeted marketing, companies are using data in a multitude of new ways. Having a DPO in place makes it more likely that the company will have GDPR controls in place. Policies, procedures, and training are more likely to be completed if a DPO is in place. The DPO can also provide warning to the business to avoid dangerous situations. A properly structured privacy program is enormously helpful in keeping your company on the right side of compliance...and avoiding fines.

3. **Less £, $ and € spent on third parties** – Recently there have been a proliferation of data experts who can help your company with all things data ... for "a small fee." From lawyers to IT Security consultants to data protection trainers, many third-parties will be keen to offer their GDPR services to your company. Having a DPO means that you have an in-house expert can provide assistance while helping you to avoid premium third-party rates.

Careless & Co. Brokers

To illustrate the entire GDPR compliance process, we're going to follow a small company struggling with GDPR compliance throughout this book. Careless & Co. provides payday loans to customers. It operates in the UK. The hero of Careless & Co. is Roger Ballentine, their information specialist. Roger was hired to help Careless & Co. prepare for GDPR. He's been anointed their DPO and is both daunted and excited by the monumental task ahead of him.

Key Points:

- Some companies are legally obligated under GDPR to appoint a DPO.
- A DPO must operate independently and report to the highest level of the company.
- You must tell Regulators and customers who your DPO is.
- Appointing a DPO may help save your company money.

Notes on Implementation

_____

_____

_____

_____

_____

_____

_____

_____

_____

_____

_____

_____

_____

_____

_____

STEP 2

Complete the Data Audit
Otherwise Known As:
Where Is All Your Data?

PINNING DOWN YOUR DATA is like nailing Jell-O to a wall. Just when you think you have it completely controlled, it slides away and you have to start all over again.

It's easy to despair when thinking about finding all of your data. But take heart – it can be done if you implement a systematic data audit process.

Introduction

To implement GDPR, you must understand where your data is and how it is being used. Our world is awash with data. In 2010 Eric Schmidt, the CEO of Google, said that: "From the dawn of civilization to 2003, five exabytes of data were created. The same amount was created in the last two days".[2]

Companies not only have data coming in from all directions, but they also share it with numerous third parties, which in turn share it with their own business partners.

In order to get to grips with all of the data you have, you are going to need to carry out a Data Protection Audit ("Data Audit").

A Data Audit is a process by which you obtain evidence about how data is being processed across your company to identify whether the company is behaving in a way that is compliant with data protection law and regulation.

Why you must carry out a Data Audit?

If your GDPR project is like building a house, then the Data Audit is laying the foundation. The Data Audit will provide you an inventory of your data, which will help you to prepare a data map and data flow diagram (more on this later).

You carry out your Data Audit to find out:

- Where your data is;
- How it is processed;
- How long you keep it;
- How secure it is;
- Where it is transferred;
- Whether there is a lawful basis (under the processing conditions) for data processing;
- What Data Protection controls you have in place; and
- What you need to do to attain GDPR compliance.

Any sizeable company is likely to carry out many Data Processing operations. For example, if a company is a bank, its data processing may include:

- Looking at huge swathes of customer data help it understand how to better sell to its products to customers and predict trends in the market (known as "Big Data analytics");
- Collecting information about customers' website browsing; and
- Sharing information with police if a customer is being investigated.

The Data Audit helps you understand how these processes are operating in order to see whether improvements need to be made. When the Data Audit is complete, the company can take action to keep it on the right side of GDPR compliance.

How thorough should my Data Audit be?

This depends on the type of the company that you work for. By the end of the Data Audit, you will have a solid idea of how your company uses data, and you can change whatever needs to be changed to comply with GDPR.

How do you carry out a Data Audit?

You can use several different tools to complete a Data Audit. Questionnaires may yield all the information you need, but you should also go talk to people to ensure you've got all the information.

Questionnaires

The first thing to do is sit down with a pad and paper and ask yourself: "How do I find out about all the data processing that is going on at my company?" You can then start preparing a Questionnaire to send out to various parts of your business.

Examples Questionnaire sections may be:

1. **Data subjects** – Whose data do we hold?
2. **Type** – Describe the type personal data that we hold. This may include name, address, medical information, credit check history, Internet browsing history, etc.

TIP: Be sure to think about data broadly. For instance, you may have customer data, supplier data, other third-party data, and employee data.

3. **Electronic** – Describe the data that is stored on our electronic systems.
4. **Paper** – Describe where we store paper data.
5. **Direct Collection** – Describe how we collect data directly from the data subject (e.g. online form, phone calls, paper forms etc.).
6. **Collection from other sources** – Do we collect any data on the data subject from other sources such as credit check databases?
7. **Privacy Notices** – What Privacy Notices do customers receive?
8. **Consent** – What consents are collected from customers from online forms or over the phone?
9. **Processing** – List the types of processing we carry out on the data (e.g., analytics on customer data, credit checks etc.).
10. **Marketing** – Describe any marketing or promotions we carry out using data.
11. **Sharing** – List with whom we share data.
12. **Third parties** – Which other third parties store our data.
13. **Transfers** – Is any of our data transferred outside the EEA? Please give details.
14. **Storage** – Give details about how and where our data is stored?
15. **Cookies** – Give details of any cookies that are used on our website.
16. **Timeliness** – How is our data kept up-to-date?
17. **Deletion** – How and when is our data deleted?
18. **Subject Rights** – How do we make sure we give effect to data subjects' rights?
19. **Controls** – What systems and controls do we have in place in relation to data (e.g. policies, staff training etc.)?

This is a non-exhaustive list, but it is a good starting point for your Data Audit.

Your Questionnaire may need to include definitions, explanations and examples. Not everyone in the business will understand the phrase "data subjects' rights." Before people start completing the Questionnaire, make sure they understand each of the questions and the terminology used. It'll save you a giant headache later because people tend to ignore things they don't understand.

Who should I send it to?

Questionnaires should be sent to someone in each department, such as sales, human resources, legal, finance, marketing, operational standards, and call centers. Make sure you send it to someone senior within the Department.

Keep in mind that you may want to tailor your Questionnaire for different roles. For instance, Human Resources is unlikely to use data for marketing purposes, so it may make sense to strip out unnecessary questions on a by-role basis.

Remember that communication is key. It is best to avoid sending emails saying, "Please complete attached Data Audit Questionnaire." Instead, try calling the people you want to answer the Questionnaire so you can preview the request.

After your call, write a follow-up email such as: *"Hi Claire, We are currently carrying out an important project to update our processes so that they are in line with the new General Data Protection Regulation. As I said on the phone today, we need your expertise in understanding how personal data is processed in your department. Would you be able to complete this by Feb 1? Let me know if you have any queries."*

What do I do next?

Once you have received the Questionnaire responses back, you should go through all of them with a highlighter pen and highlight the areas that:

- Require further information; and
- Pose a potential risk to your company.

It is a good idea to arrange to meet each person who completed a Questionnaire so that you can obtain further information on any issue they raised.

Careless & Co.

Careless & Co.'s DPO Roger Ballentine sets out to complete his Data Audit by drafting a Questionnaire.

Careless & Co. is a small company, so Roger sends the Questionnaire to the head of sales, marketing, information technology, information security, and legal.

Roger's Questionnaire looks like this:

1. What types of people do you hold personal information about (e.g. customers, employees, suppliers)?	2. Please list the types of personal data you hold about customers (e.g. name, address, contact details, occupation, medical information relating to their loan application).	3. Please list the data you hold on employees and any other people.
4. What electronic data do you hold on your computer systems?	5. Is this data held on a central computer system or on your own personal computer?	6. What security do you have in relation to the data on your computer systems?
7. Who has access to the data on your computers?	8. Is there any record of who accesses the data held on the office computers?	9. Has data held on the office computers ever been lost or accessed when it shouldn't have been? Please give details.

10. Is any data held on paper? Please give details.	11. Where is your paper data stored?	12. Do you destroy old paper documents? Please give details.
13. Please describe when you collect data directly from customers (i.e. when they come into the shop, fill out loan forms, give details over the phone etc.).	14. Please describe when you collect data on customers from third parties (e.g. credit check databases, loan guarantors, customer's employers etc.).	15. Do customers receive any information from you about how their information will be used? Such as information on your webpage or in their loan documents?
16. What do you do with the customer's information (e.g. process loan applications, check the customer's credit history, send funds, collect payments on the loan, send marketing materials, process legal documents when customers have defaulted on the loan, store customer's information etc.)?	17. Do you send the customers any information about marketing or promotions? If so, please describe. Can the customer opt-out of receiving these offers and promotions?	18. Do you ask for the customer's permission to send offers and promotions?
19. Is any data sent outside Europe? Please give details of all such countries.	20. Please describe how and when data is deleted.	21. Do you know of any instances when we share customer data with any other company (e.g. credit check companies, cloud storage companies, marketing companies, people-tracing companies, external lawyers)?

22. Can the customer see his/her data if s/he wants to?	23. Has any customer ever complained about how his/her data is used?	24. Are you aware of any company policies or guidance in relation to how we you allowed to use data?
25. Have you received any training in relation to using data?	26. Do you hold any data about employees? If so, please describe.	27. Where is it stored?
28. Who has access to the staff data?	29. Please describe the building security at your office.	30. Are there any aspects of our data use or storage about which you have concerns?

Now It's Your Turn:

Fill in this starter questionnaire to get you thinking about your own full Questionnaire.

Note: As you fill in the exercises throughout the book, the answers you give may contain highly sensitive information. You'll want to keep this book secured or answer the questions separately in a password-protected file.

1. What types of people do you hold personal information about (e.g. customers, employees, suppliers)?	2. Please list the types of personal data you hold about customers (e.g. name, address, contact details, occupation, medical information relating to their loan application).	3. Please list the data you hold on employees and any other people.
4. What electronic data do you hold on your computer systems?	5. Is this data held on a central computer system or on your own personal computer?	6. What security do you have in relation to the data on your computer systems?

7. Who has access to the data on your computers?	8. Is there any record of who accesses the data held on the office computers?	9. Has data held on the office computers ever been lost or accessed when it shouldn't have been? Please give details.
10. Is any data held on paper? Please give details.	11. Where is your paper data stored?	12. Do you destroy old paper documents? Please give details.
13. Please describe when you collect data directly from customers (i.e. when they come into the shop, fill out loan forms, give details over the phone etc.).	14. Please describe when you collect data on customers from third parties (e.g. credit check databases, loan guarantors, customer's employers etc.).	15. Do customers receive any information from you about how their information will be used? Such as information on your webpage or in their loan documents?

16. What do you do with the customer's information (e.g. process loan applications, check the customer's credit history, send funds, collect payments on the loan, send marketing materials, process legal documents when customers have defaulted on the loan, store customer's information etc.)?	17. Do you send the customers any information about marketing or promotions? If so, please describe. Can the customer opt-out of receiving these offers and promotions?	18. Do you ask for the customer's permission to send offers and promotions?
19. Is any data sent outside Europe? Please give details of all such coun-tries.	20. Please describe how and when data is deleted.	21. Do you know of any instances when we share customer data with any other company (e.g. credit check companies, cloud storage companies, marketing companies, people-tracing companies, external lawyers)?
22. Can the customer see his/her data if s/he wants to?	23. Has any customer ever complained about how his/her data is used?	24. Are you aware of any company policies or guidance in relation to how we you allowed to use data?

25. Have you received any training in relation to using data?	26. Do you hold any data about employees? If so, please describe.	27. Where is it stored?
28. Who has access to the staff data?	29. Please describe the building security at your office.	30. Are there any aspects of our data use or storage about which you have concerns?

To whom will you direct the Questionnaire? Send it to as many relevant departments as possible.

Title	Name	Email Address

Key Points:

- **Audit needed** – You need to carry out a Data Audit to better understand what your company is doing with its data and what GDPR risks are present.
- **Questionnaire** – You should prepare a Questionnaire that asks for details on how data is processed.
- **Send it out** – The Questionnaire should be sent to all departments of the company that carry out data processing.
- **Follow up with meetings** – When you receive the completed Questionnaires you should review them and follow up with in-person meetings to ensure you properly understand how data is processed.

Once you've finished your Data Audit, you're going to need a way to aggregate and organize all of the information. That's where Step 3 comes in – mapping your data flows.

Notes on Implementation

STEP 3

Make Your Data Map

LIKE A TREASURE MAP, only more valuable – your Data Map is a critical tool in understanding how data flows into and out of your business. Your Data Audit will yield a wealth of information, but the information isn't organized. Raw data from a Data Audit tends to look like a bowl of spaghetti. You know data comes and goes from one point to another, but it's hard to find the start and end-point, or to see clearly where it goes.

The answer to this prickly problem is to map out the data. By seeing where each type of data starts, moves and ends, you can get a grip on what's happening, which helps you to understand what your company is doing with data and what needs fixing. A Data Map will help you move through the next steps more smoothly.

Preparing a report on your Data Audit

Now that you've completed your Data Audit, you should prepare a written report summarizing how data is used across your company. The repot should include details about how the processing that is carried out. Share the results with Legal, Compliance, and anyone else who should know about your data use.

Mapping your data flows

To begin the data mapping process, you need to understand the data flows in your business. This means understanding:

- How data flows into the company
- How we share it internally
- Who has access to it
- Who we share it with
- Whether we are transferring any data abroad

The next step is to prepare a visual map of the flows to help you understand these processes.

Careless & Co.

Roger Ballentine was pleased to get back all the Questionnaires he sent out as part of the Data Audit. He pulls together his notes from the follow-up calls he made, and now is ready to draft his data map. Here's how it looks:

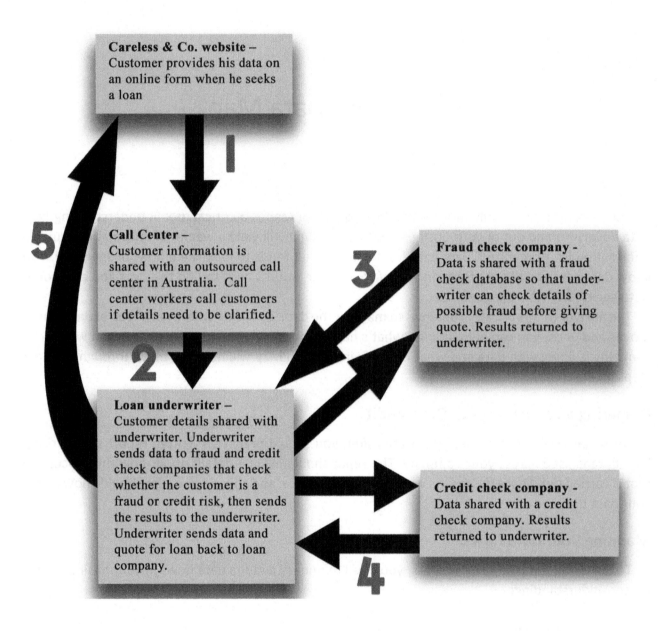

Roger immediately notices that there may be issues with how data is being used, stored and transferred. Roger knows he will need to find out about:

- **Data going to Australia** – Roger knows that ensuring proper contractual clauses are in place with the Australian call center provider is a top priority.
- **Data Security** – Roger needs to verify how third parties like the Australian call center and underwriter are keeping the data secure.

- **Adequate Disclosure** – Roger needs to ensure that customers have adequate knowledge of the checks that are done on the data. He will review Careless & Co.'s Privacy Notice today.

Roger makes notes on these issues so he can work on them throughout the GDPR readiness process.

Now It's Your Turn

Your map may be significantly simpler or more complex than Careless & Co.'s. Begin drawing your data map here:

What questions or issues does your data map bring up? Note them here:

1._____

_____

2._____

_____

3._____

_____

4._____

_____

5._____

_____

6._____

_____

Preparing the Risk Register

After your data mapping exercise is done, it's time to prepare your Risk Register.

What is a risk register?

A risk register is a form or a document that sets out the different data privacy risks your company faces.

For example, if you work in a marketing company and you find out the company is sending spam emails to people on behalf of a retail company without the customer's consent, you would:

- Note this on your risk register as a key risk;
- Decide how risky this spam email practice is by giving it a score (e.g. from 1-10 or from low to high); and
- Describe what you need to do next to deal with the risk (e.g. warn the board of how dangerous it is, look toward obtaining customer consents where you are able to etc.).

What should my Risk Register include?

The Risk Register should detail:

- The major risks regarding how your data is used;
- The aspects of processing that could potentially breach GDPR; and
- Details of what you need to do next.

Your Risk Register might look like this:

Data Processing	Carried out by	Risk Rating	Potential Breaches of GDPR?	Next steps
Sending marketing emails to customers with vague consents	Marketing Department	High	Marketing emails sent without proper consents may note meet the requirements of Article 6(1)(a) of the GDPR	Change all consents to ensure they are sufficient and allow customer to withdraw consent Train Marketing team

Careless & Co.'s Risk Register

Roger took the results of his Data Audit and his Data Map to make Careless & Co.'s Risk Register:

Data Processing	Carried out by	Risk Rating	Potential Breaches of GDPR?	Next steps
Sending marketing emails to customers and others with vague consents	Head of sales	High	Marketing emails are being sent without proper consents	Change all consents to ensure they are sufficient and allow customer to withdraw consent Train Marketing team
CCTV footage collected of employees working and people on the street outside the office with no signage telling people about the recording	Head of security	High	Risk that the first principle in relation to fair, lawful and transparent data processing has been breached	Suspend CCTV while we consider how to carry out less invasive form of building security
No entrance security or visitors register kept	Head of security	High	Risk to GDPR principle to keep data secure. Inadequate controls around building makes data less secure	Audit access to the building and man reception desk. Tighten security around the building generally

Data Processing	Carried out by	Risk Rating	Potential Breaches of GDPR?	Next steps
Data passed to marketing companies to help analyze which customers to target in future	Head of sales	Moder-ate	We obtain customer consents to this on our online forms and we make sure that we only use data where we have obtained consents	Check that our consents are good enough and check that we do not use any data where customers have not consented
No information given to customers about how we use their data on our websites or our documents	Legal	High	This breaches GDPR in terms of using data fairly, lawfully and transparently	Draft Privacy Notice for websites and customer documents to explain to them how we use their data
Staff are not trained on how to use data	Legal	High	This potentially breaches GDPR in relation to ensuring data is kept securely	Prepare online training module and provide face-to-face sessions with Legal, Sales, Information Technology, and Human Resources

Now It's Your Turn

Begin your Risk Registry by jotting down your initial thoughts on where your risks lie.

Data Processing	Carried out by	Risk Rating	Potential Breaches of GDPR?	Next steps

Key Points:

- **Map the data flows** – Drawing a map of the data flows will help you pinpoint the issues.
- **Prepare a Data Audit report** – When the Data Audit is complete, you should prepare a report about how data is processed within your company.
- **Prepare a Risk Register** – You should prepare a Risk Register that outlines:
  - The major risks inherent in the way data is being used;
  - How these activities could breach GDPR;
  - What you need to do next.

Now that your data audit and data mapping are complete, let's turn to the most important task of all: securing the ship.

Notes on Implementation

STEP 4

Get Straight on Security

I WANT YOU TO THINK about your company as a cruise ship for a moment. Making sure you have adequate data security in place is like making sure your cruise ship is watertight. All of the other secondary jobs on the ship, such as polishing the brass and stocking the bar, become pointless if the ship is leaking.

On a ship, there are many layers of security. There are obvious actions like ensuring only ticketed passengers board the ship. There are lifeboats in case something goes wrong, and drills to ensure passengers know how to leave quickly in the event of an emergency. But there are also subtle features at work, like security cameras being watched deep below deck to ensure the safety of all passengers.

Like a ship in choppy waters, all the other tasks become futile if you do not tackle the fundamental issue of water-tightness and security. If you do not handle data security, many of your other GDPR tasks are merely rearranging the deckchairs as the ship slowly sinks.

If you remember any phrase from this book then let it be this:

Assuring data security stops the big problems that can hurt me.

What does GDPR say about Data Security?

Article 5(f) of the GDPR says data must be "processed in a manner that ensures appropriate security of the personal data, including protection against unauthorized or unlawful processing and against accidental loss, destruction or damage, using appropriate technical or organizational measures." Article 32 gives more detail on this and explains that the greater the damage that could be caused to customers by a data breach, the greater the effort you have to make to keep the data secure.

The GDPR ups the ante in several ways when it comes to data security. For instance:

- Huge fines can be levied against companies for data breaches;
- Processors can now be punished if they do not keep data secure; and
- There is a mandatory requirement to report data breaches (see Step 9 - Reporting Data Breaches).

Great – But what do I have to do?

Unfortunately, there is no one answer when it comes to data security. Rather, there are a number of areas to be considered. Like much of the rest of your GDPR project, data security is something that requires continuous maintenance and consistent improvement. This means that we need to constantly monitor our data security and be vigilant for new threats.

Consequences

There has been much talk about the maximum fines under GDPR. However, the consequences of inadequate Data Security do not stop at regulator fines. Remember Target, the U.S. retail giant that suffered a hack of forty million customers' credit card details in 2013?

The Target breach is the one that strikes fear into the hearts of DPOs across the globe. How did it happen? Well, appears that hackers gained access to the Target systems through one of its air conditioning suppliers. It was reported that the hackers tricked one of the supplier's employees into clicking a malicious email. Seemingly, this vendor enjoyed wide and unnecessary access privileges to Target's systems. From there the hackers got the keys to Target's kingdom and were able to access 40 million people's details.[3]

Target suffered years of adverse publicity and litigation, which hit their share price and their finances hard. The cost of Target's mistake: a reported $202 million.[4]

This is one of the more famous data breaches of all time and it resulted in the resignations of both the CEO and the Chief Information Officer.

Inspecting the ship

Before you can move on to tackling the data security issues you face you must first find your vulnerabilities.

You need to investigate your current data security before you can make improvements to your systems and controls.

How do you go about inspecting the ship? It is a good idea to prepare a table that helps you understand what your data security issues are. Your Data Audit can help with this.

Below is an example Data Security Table that can help you to assess your existing data security:

Data Security Issue	Questions	Answers
Building Security	<ul><li>Is the building secure?</li><li>Could members of the public get access to customer data?</li><li>Is CCTV in place?</li><li>Is there a record of who gets into the building?</li></ul>	

Data Security Issue	Questions	Answers
Computer systems	• Are software updates installed regularly? • Do your systems monitor for unusual activity? • Is your data backed up? • Do you use breach detection technology?	
Employees	• Do employees receive any training on data security? • Do employees know how to report a data breach to the DPO? • What access do employees have to customer data?	
Policies and Procedures	• Do you have adequate policies and procedures in place?	
Third parties	• Which third parties have access to our data? • Are there contracts in place to ensure that third parties behave when they are handling our data?	

I know this table seems intimidating. But with data security, we all have to start looking at our ship to see if there is any vulnerability, so we can plug the leaks.

Careless & Co.'s Data Security Table

Let's see how our friends at Careless & Co. are doing with their data security.

Data Security Issue	Questions	Answers
Building Security	• Is the building secure? • Could members of the public get access to customer data? • Is CCTV in place? • Is there a record of who enters the building?	• Unmanned reception desk. No security • Many paper files with unlocked filing cabinets • No security passes • No record of who enters the building • CCTV of car park only
Computer systems	• Are software updates installed regularly? • Do your systems monitor for unusual activity? • Is your data backed up? • Do you use breach detection technology?	• IT Dept. under-resourced with no software updates carried out • Some sporadic monitoring • Data backed up once a year • No breach detection
Employees	• Do employees receive any training on data security? • Do employees know how to report a data breach to the DPO? • What access do employees have to customer data?	• Employees received online data protection training module once per year. No training records kept • No training on reporting data breaches • All 134 employees have unrestricted access to all customer data
Policies and Procedures	• Do you have adequate policies and procedures in place?	• One Data Protection Policy. Last updated in 2001
Third parties	• Which third parties have access to our data? • Are there contracts in place to ensure that third parties behave when they are handling our data?	• Outsourced IT providers have access to all of our customer data • Some contracts in place with suppliers but none cover data protection issues

Now it's Your Turn

It's your turn to have a go at completing the Data Security Table for your company. If you have issues in addition to the ones in the table, you can use the template to draft a fuller table with more topics that relate to you. As this Data Security Table is likely to contain very sensitive information, you may want to copy this table onto your PC before you complete the answers.

Data Security Issue	Questions	Answers
Building Security	• Is the building secure? • Could members of the public get access to customer data? • Is CCTV in place? • Is there a record of who gets into the building?	
Computer systems	• Are software updates installed regularly? • Do your systems monitor for unusual activity? • Is your data backed up? • Do you use breach detection technology? •	
Employees	• Do employees receive any training on data security? • Do employees know how to report a data breach to the DPO? • What access do employees have to customer data?	
Policies and Procedures	• Do you have adequate policies and procedures in place?	

Data Security Issue	Questions	Answers
Third parties	• Which third parties have access to our data? • Are there contracts in place to ensure third parties behave when they are handling our data?	
[Other Topic]_____		
[Other Topic]_____		
[Other Topic]_____		

What do I do once I have inspected the ship?

In GDPR, as in life, we need to prioritize. This means that you should decide which of your data security issues pose the greatest risks, and respond to those first. For example, if you discover there are vast swathes of sensitive personal data being sent out of your company unencrypted on a daily basis, then this would be a vulnerability that needs fixed urgently.

How do you know which vulnerabilities create the biggest threat? You should prioritize the issues relating to (1) where you are processing the largest amount of data or (2) the most sensitive (known as "special categories" of data under GDPR). Remember, the greater the potential damage a breach could cause to customers, the greater the effort you have to take to keep that data secure. For example, a company operating an online dating service must have more security around customer dating preferences than the security it has around list of where its employees park in the staff parking lot.

Remember, the greater the potential damage a breach could cause to customers, the greater the effort you have to take to keep that data secure.

Just like the ship – it won't much matter if someone stole another person's jewelry if the iceberg has torn a hole in the hull. You should fix the biggest holes in the ship first.

Ranking the Risk

To determine which risk to prioritize, you'll need to give each one a score, then rank them from highest to lowest. Assign each issue a score from 1 (low risk / small use of personal data and no use of sensitive personal data) to 10 (high amounts of personal data and/or use of sensitive personal data), then put the risks in order from highest to lowest.

Careless & Co.

Now that Careless & Co. has a completed Data Security Table, it's time for Roger to assign a number to each area of risk.

Data Security Issue	Questions	Answers	Priority of Concern (1-10)
Building Security	• Is the building secure? • Could members of the public get access to customer data? • Is CCTV in place? • Is there a record of who enters the building?	• Unmanned reception desk. No security • Many paper files with unlocked filing cabinets • No security passes • No record of who enters the building • CCTV of car park only	5
Computer systems	• Are software updates installed regularly? • Do your systems monitor for unusual activity? • Is your data backed up? • Do you use breach detection technology?	• IT Dept. under-resourced with no software updates carried out • Some sporadic monitoring • Data backed up once a year • No breach detection	10

Data Security Issue	Questions	Answers	Priority of Concern (1-10)
Employees	• Do employees receive any training on data security? • Do employees know how to report a data breach to the DPO? • What access do employees have to customer data?	• Employees received online data protection training module once per year. No training records kept • No training on reporting data breaches • All 134 employees have unrestricted access to all customer data	8
Policies and Procedures	• Do you have adequate policies and procedures in place?	• One Data Protection Policy. Last updated in 2001	7
Third parties	• Which third parties have access to our data? • Are there contracts in place to ensure that third parties behave when they are handling our data?	• Outsourced IT providers have access to all of our customer data • Some contracts in place with suppliers but none cover data protection issues	9

Roger tabulated the scores and ranked his risk areas as follows:

1. Computer Systems
2. Third Parties
3. Employees
4. Policies and Procedures
5. Building Security

Based on his risk ranking, Roger decided to draft a plan to secure the computer systems first. While the other risks continue to be important, Roger knows that he should start with updating the computer systems and then begin working on restricting third-party access to customer data.

Now it's Your Turn

Using the Data Security Table you created above, score each area of risk until you have a ranking of the highest risk issues. Assign each issue a score from 1 (low risk / small use of personal data and no use of sensitive personal data) to 10 (high amounts of personal data and/or use of sensitive personal data).

Data Security Issue	Questions	Answers	Priority of Concern (1-10)
Computer systems	• Are software updates installed regularly? • Do your systems monitor for unusual activity? • Is your data backed up? • Do you use breach detection technology?		
Employees	• Do employees receive training on data security? • Do employees know how to report a data breach to the DPO? • What access do employees have to customer data?		
Policies and Procedures	• Do you have adequate policies and procedures in place?		
Third parties	• Which third parties have access to our data? • Are there contracts in place to ensure that third parties behave when they are handling our data?		

Data Security Issue	Questions	Answers	Priority of Concern (1-10)
[Other Topic]_____	•		
[Other Topic]_____	•		
[Other Topic]_____	•		

Don't get daunted

After you have inspected the boat, you may want to abandon ship. Don't be daunted! Once you know the state of play, the real work can begin. And remember, by plugging the holes now, you protect against greater problems later.

Data breaches can happen in many different ways, including:

- Employee mistakes
- Equipment failure
- Hacking
- Blagging (i.e. con artists contacting the company and pretending to be someone else)
- Malware (software designed to gain access to your systems)
- Loss of equipment

It is impossible for any sizeable company to have perfect data security. It is, however, possible to find where the main gaps are so you can urgently fix the leaks and lessen the chance of any customer data going into the wild.

Cyber Insurance

Make sure your company has adequate insurance in place to cover you against the effects of a major data breach. GDPR creates more exposure for companies than ever before in the area of fines, liabilities, and litigation. You need to make sure your company is protected against the harsher effects of GDPR by having cyber insurance in place. In short, make sure the ship has lifeboats.

Figuring out whether you have adequate cyber insurance can be complex, and you may wish to take advice from insurance experts or lawyers. Review your current policies see what level of cover you have. If your cyber insurance only covers the cost of fixing your systems in the event of a data breach, you could be exposed to millions of dollars in litigation costs and fines.

What do I do now?

Data security can be highly technical area that could merit a collection of books in itself. However, there are three areas of concern you should always consider.

(1) Plugging the Leaks – The staff

Staff are the widely considered to be the most common cause of data breaches.
Make sure your staff is trained to keep data secure by focusing on topics such as:

- What to do if there is a data breach;
- How to transfer data securely both inside and outside the office;
- How to work securely from home;
- How to comply with your company Data Protection Policy;
- How to avoid falling victim to malware, phishing, and blagging attacks;
- Being careful with company information on social media;
- Setting proper passwords;
- The maximum penalties under the GDPR;
- How to report a data breach to the DPO's email address or a hotline See Step 7 – Get on the Training Train for further information.

(2) Plugging the Leaks – Cybersecurity

Cybersecurity includes the technology, policies, and procedures you have in place to protect your data against cyber crimes such as hacking or ransom attacks.

Cybersecurity is essential to GDPR compliance. The biggest Regulator fine to date in the UK (against TalkTalk in October 2015) was imposed due to cybersecurity failure. The Information Commissioner's Office fined TalkTalk £400,000 for inadequate website security. TalkTalk had not updated their database software adequately which led to hackers being able to attack the website and steal the data of almost 157,000 customers.[5]

Make sure your cybersecurity is in good shape across the company.

Top Tips:

- **Breach detection** – Some cybersecurity breaches happen for months or even years before the company becomes aware. Cyber criminals can be subtle operators. Make sure the Information Technology and Security people in your company have implemented proper breach detection technology so that they would be alerted of a cyber attack at the earliest opportunity.
- **Software patches** – Software applications must be updated regularly to ensure that flaws in security are remediated. If your software needs updating, it means that there is vulnerability, and the ship may be leaking. Fix it.
- **Penetration Testing** – Carry out regular "pen tests" (penetration testing) of your network to ensure you fix the weak spots before hackers exploit them.

- **Encryption** – Encrypting data when it is stored and when it is in transit can mitigate against the worst effects of hackers. You should consider using a risk-based approach to determine which of your data should be encrypted. It is always wise to have an Encryption Policy in place.

(3) Plugging the Leaks – The Data Breach Response Plan.

Suffering a data breach such as a hack is inevitable for most companies.

"There are only two types of companies: those that have been hacked and those that will be." – Former FBI Director Robert Mueller[6]

Your company is going to need a Data Breach Response Plan in place so it knows how to respond if a cyber attack or any other type of data breach that occurs. We cover data breach planning in Step 9 – What to Do When It All Goes Wrong: Preparing for and Reporting Data Breaches but for now, just know that having a data breach plan is a critical part of data security.

Key Points:

- Data Security is the most important part of GDPR compliance.
- Inspect your ship.
- Train your staff.
- Make sure you have adequate cybersecurity.
- Put a Data Breach Response Plan in place.
- Get Cyber insured.

Now that we know we're running a tight ship that's ship-shape, it's time to let the world know what we're doing with their data.

Notes on Implementation

_____

_____

_____

_____

_____

_____

_____

_____

_____

_____

_____

_____

_____

_____

_____

_____

_____

STEP 5

Tell it Like it Is with Privacy Notices

QUIZ: HOW LONG DO YOU normally spend reading an online, pop-up privacy notice before you scroll to the bottom to find the "I Accept" button?

a. Twenty minutes
b. One minute
c. As fast as I can
d. I've never tried to read them at all, I simply click "I Accept"

If you're anything like most consumers, the answer is either C or D. Privacy Notices have become ubiquitous and imposing. Does it have to be this way? Could there be value to companies in explaining what they do with their customers' data in a more interesting way? Could transparency be a benefit to commerce? I think so, but before that can happen, we need to re-think privacy notices.

What is a Privacy Notice?

A Privacy Notice is the way in which you tell customers (or other data subjects – I use "customers" for ease of reference) about how you use their data.

Examples of different types of Privacy Notices are:

- An online Privacy "policy" or notice on a website;
- A paragraph about how your information is used in your pension documents; or
- A company giving you information over the phone about calls being recorded.

The main Privacy Notice or what I like to think of as the "Master" Privacy Notice is the customer-facing Internet Privacy Notice. All of your other Privacy Notices should be shorted versions of the Master Privacy Notice document, and any shortened version must be consistent with the Master document.

What does GDPR say about Privacy Notices?

Under Article 5 of GDPR we must use data fairly, lawfully and transparently. Under Articles 13 and 14, customers also have the right to be informed about how their data is used. This is why companies need Privacy Notices. A company may be breaching GDPR if it does not inform customers about what it is doing with their data.

Rules about Privacy Notices can be found in Articles 12, 13, and 14 of GDPR. GDPR requires that Privacy Notices be understandable, accessible, and written in plain language.

The information in Privacy Notices must always be made available to the customer free of charge.

Is there anything I have to include?

Under GDPR there are certain things the Privacy Notice must contain, including:

- The identity and contact details of your company and the DPO;
- The reasons for processing the customer's data and the legal basis for doing so;
- The categories of data you are processing (you do not need to include this if you are collecting the information directly from the customer);
  - o "Categories of data" means the types of personal data that you are processing. For example, a company might be using a customer's name, address, email address, credit check details and details about the customer's health in order to decide whether to provide the customer with healthcare.
- Source of the data;
- Who it might be disclosed to;
- Details of where it might be going in the world (i.e. international transfers);
- How long we keep the data, and details about the customer's rights;
- Whether the customer is legally or contractually required to provide it and the consequences if they refuse to provide it;
- Details about profiling that may be carried out (See The introduction for more details on profiling); and
- Information on the right to lodge a complaint with a Regulator.

When do I need to give the Privacy Notice to the customer?

Under GDPR there are some technical rules about when you must provide privacy notification information to the customer.

- If you are collecting the data directly from the customer, then you need to give her privacy-related information at the time you are obtaining the data. For example, if a customer is completing an online form, she should be able to see the Privacy Notice at the time of completion.
- If you are getting the customer data from a third party, you need to give privacy-related information to the customer either:
  - o Within a reasonable period, or one month at the latest; OR
  - o If the data is to be used to communicate with the customer, you must give it to her as soon as you communicate with her; OR
  - o If the data obtained from the third party is going to be given to a fourth party, you must give the Privacy Notice to her before you give her data to the fourth party.

How much detail should we include in the Privacy Notice?

We do not need to include every tiny detail in the Privacy Notice. If something is perfectly obvious, it does not need to go in.

For example, if I order a book on Amazon, do I really need to be told that they might pass my details to a courier in order that they can deliver it to my apartment in London? Probably not.

But if I am buying a movie news app and the app owner plans to carry out big data analytics using my data, should I be told of this in the Privacy Notice? Most definitely. Big data analytics is a much more controversial practice, and I deserve to know this.

Where do I start?

Before you start drafting your Privacy Notices, you need a good idea about what is happening with data in your organization. Pull out your completed Data Audit and Data Map from Steps 1 and 2. They'll help you to complete the exercise.

You'll want to draft your Master Privacy Notice (the customer-facing Internet Privacy Policy) first. To do this, we need to come up with a Privacy Notice Plan.

Your Privacy Notice Plan will be divided into three main sections:

- How we collect your information;
- What we do with it; and
- Who we share it with.

Careless & Co.'s Privacy Notice Plan

Roger, Careless & Co.'s DPO, knows he needs to draft his Master Privacy Policy. His Privacy Notice Plan looks like this:

How we collect customer information	What we do with the customer information	Who we share customer information with
• We buy data about our customers from a marketing company • We collect data about our customers' online behavior on our website via cookies • We record calls with our customers • We collect credit card information and contact details when customers purchase items via our website • We collect information from our customers when they enter competitions and promotions or complete surveys for us	• We use customer data for big data projects • We sell customer data to marketing companies • We use customer details to fulfill their orders • We store their details on our U.S. servers • We text and email customers about our offers and promotions • We use customer information to send pop up ads on our website	• Credit check companies • Marketing analytics companies • Our IT service providers • Our cloud providers • Our call center service providers • Our survey companies • Marketing companies to whom we sell data • Payment service providers • Website advertising companies that assist us with pop-up ads

Now it's Your Turn

To draft your Privacy Notice Plan, use the table below to document how you collect information, what you do with it and with whom you share it. As this table may contain sensitive information, be sure to keep the book in a safe place.

How we collect customer information (e.g. online forms, recorded phone calls, postal applications)	What we do with the customer information (e.g. customer administration, marketing emails, storage)	Who we share customer information with (e.g. our couriers, credit check companies)

Drafting Your Privacy Notice

Now that you've written your Privacy Notice Plan, it's time to start drafting. Review your Privacy Notice Plan to find out what you need to communicate to customers about how your company uses their data.

Tips on Privacy Notice Drafting

Pascal famously said, "I'm sorry I wrote you such a long letter; I didn't have time to write a short one."

Under GDPR, the onus is on companies to COMMUNICATE properly with customers. Top 5 tips on communicating properly with customers in the Privacy Notice:

- **Keep it short** - There is a skill in making a long, complex document into a shorter document without cutting the substance.
- A good Privacy Notice should run to no more than two or three pages. It is hard to think of an organization that collects and processes more data than Google. Yet their Privacy Notice is masterful in its brevity. It runs two and a half pages.
- **Avoid jargon** – Remember there is an obligation under GDPR to have Privacy Notices "written in clear and plain language." They also must be "accessible" and "concise."
- **Use short sentences** – Keep your sentences short. Most sentences should not be longer than fifteen words, and they should only express one thought at a time.
- **Presentation** – Set the Privacy Notice out in an attractive way. The structure should be simple and obvious with headings such as: The information we collect. How we use your information. How we share your information etc.

- **Tone** - Try and adopt the tone of an honest guide. The tone of too many Privacy Notices is that of an airport security guard rather than that of a helpful friend. It is better to explain gently rather than dictate to customers in patronizing terms.

For example, let's say a Privacy Notice needs to advise employees that their emails are being monitored.

A good way of communicating this might be: *"We pay attention to how our computer systems are used at work. This includes checking that employees are using email in an appropriate way. For more details click here www.AcmeStaffHandbook.com."*

A poor example might be *"We hereby advise you that all email activity will be strictly monitored and inappropriate or criminal behavior will be censured and reported to law enforcement where necessary. Failure to abide by the email policy may lead to consequences up to and including termination of employment."* The latter is unlikely to win the trust of employees!

Careless & Co.'s Privacy Policy

Roger uses his Privacy Notice Plan to draft his Master Privacy Notice. He writes it in three separate paragraphs for ease of comprehension.

Paragraph 1: How we collect your information

We collect your information when you complete our online forms, purchase our products over the phone, enter our competitions and complete our surveys. We also buy information about you from third-party marketing companies. We collect data that we obtain using cookies on our website. We record all of the discussions we have with you on the phone. The information we collect includes your name, address, email address, credit card details, credit history, and health information.

Paragraph 2: What we do with it

We use your information to send you the products you have ordered from us online or on the phone. We sell your data (apart from your credit card details) to marketing companies. We use your data in big data projects to help us understand trends in the marketplace. Depending on the product your order, we may check your credit history. We use your information to send you marketing emails containing special offers and promotions run by Careless & Co. and our approved business partners. We store your information on our servers in the UK and the US. We also may store your information with our cloud service providers in Australia. We use cookies to monitor your behavior when you are on our website including details about how you clicked through to our site, how long you spend on each of the pages of our site, and whether you responded to any pop-up ads we may send to you on our site.

Paragraph 3: Whom we share it with

We share your details with other companies in our group and with our selected business partners. These business partners may include:

- Cloud Providers that help us store your information
- IT service providers that help us with our internal IT issues

- Marketing analytics companies that give us insight on who is buying our products in order that we can more effectively sell our products
- Payment service providers that process your payment information on our behalf
- Companies that help us send you targeted pop-up ads when you are on our site
- Credit check companies that help us understand your credit history
- Survey companies that help us to send you surveys to understand your experience of our services
- Couriers that help deliver our products to you
- Lawyers representing us in the event of a legal claim
- Regulators and law enforcement agencies (if there is a legal reason to share your data with them)
- Search engine operators that help us understand how to improve our visibility online

Now It's Your Turn:

Use your Privacy Notice Plan to make a first draft of your Privacy Notice. It doesn't have to be perfect, but it does need to communicate:

- How we collect your information
- What we do with it
- Who we share it with.

Paragraph 1: How we collect your information

_____
_____
_____
_____
_____
_____
_____

Paragraph 2: What we do with it

_____
_____
_____
_____
_____
_____
_____

Paragraph 3: Whom we share it with

_____

_____

_____

_____

_____

_____

_____

Should we consider using a layered Privacy Notice?

Many companies are using layered privacy notices. Layered privacy notices allow the customer to see a shortened version of the Privacy Notice in various places, with a link or information explaining how to obtain the full version if they want more details on how their information is used.

For example, on a mobile app, you can show the customer the short version of the Privacy Notice because you do not have much space with which to communicate privacy information. A link can be provided to click-through to the complete Privacy Notice. Or, if a customer is applying for a department store credit card online, they may see the following short Privacy Notice:

"We collect your information when you complete our application for a credit card. We store this information on our system. We use information about your credit card use to record what you purchase in our store. We share your information with business partners such as delivery companies and credit check companies. Our full privacy policy may be found at www. ACMEstoresandcards.com/privacynotice. "

How many Privacy Notices do we need?

Like so much of data privacy law, there is no hard and fast rule. We must use our judgment to determine how we can best communicate with customers about how we use their information.

A (Customer's) Journey of A Thousand Miles Begins with the First Step

Perhaps you have heard the term "customer journey?" The customer journey is the number of times the customer has contact with a company throughout his or her lifetime as the company's customer. During various parts of the customer journey, you will want to give the customer differing privacy-related information.

Let's say a customer named Panos wants to buy car insurance. When Panos buys and uses his car insurance policy, he goes through the following experiences:

Stage 1. Buying the policy online;

Stage 2. Receiving his insurance documents in the post;

Stage 3. Calling the insurance company to make a claim when his car is stolen; and

Stage 4. Completing a claim form to process the claim on his insurance policy.

Let's follow Panos' customer's journey to see if we should give him information about how his data is used at each stage of the journey.

Panos visits your company's website and finds a great deal on car insurance. He decides to buy the policy online.

Stage 1: Buying the Product online. It would be appropriate to let Panos see your full Privacy Notice giving complete details of how his information is used when he first buys the product online.

Panos feels good about buying the policy, but he isn't sure about all of the details and he only glanced at the full Privacy Notice when he was online. He is therefore happy to receive documents in the mail reminding him of the intricacies of his car insurance policy in case he needs to retrieve them.

Stage 2: Receiving documents in the mail. It would be helpful if Panos received a short summary of the Privacy Notice in the documents you mail.

Panos realizes that he needs to add another driver to his policy after his wife sells her car. He calls the customer call center to make this change.

Stage 3: Talking to the company on the phone. The call center operative should tell Panos whether the call is being recorded.

Six months after buying his insurance, another driver reverses into Panos' car at a supermarket parking lot. He visits a body shop to get the car fixed and he makes a claim on his insurance to pay for the car repairs.

Stage 4: Completing a claim form to make a claim on his insurance policy. The company should include a brief statement on the claim form about what they will do with the data Panos provides. For example, the company may share the information with fraud investigators and Panos should know this.

Consider your own customer journey to determine when you should give the customer information about how you use his/her data.

Remember you do NOT have to include Privacy Notice information every time you interact with the customer.

Privacy Policies and Employees

Don't forget that you need a separate Privacy Notice for employees to instruct employees on (1) how your company collects their information, (2) what the company does with it and (3) with whom the company shares it. You can put this Privacy Notice in your Staff Handbook or intranet page.

For example, a Privacy Notice may need to advise employees in the staff handbook that their emails are being monitored. The Privacy Notice to the employees may read as follows:

"We pay attention to how our computer systems are used at work. This includes checking that employees are using emails in the appropriate way. We observe emails for the use of inappropriate language and keeping an eye on emails that are sent outside our company to make sure that our employees are behaving in a manner that is consistent with our company policies. For more details click here www.AcmeStaffHandbook.com."

Key Points:

- Some matters are required within Privacy Notices under GDPR (such as the contact details of the company and the DPO);
- You do not need to include every detail in the Privacy Notice;
- Layered is good;
- Keep it short and clear, avoid jargon, present it well, and use an appropriate tone.

Now that we've communicated with our customers, it's time put it in writing with our Staff Policies.

Notes on Implementation

STEP 6

Get it in Writing – Staff Policies

ASK MANY COMPANIES WHERE their staff policies ("policies") are and you will be taken to the darkest corner of the basement, lead to a dust-covered box, and asked to turn on your flashlight so you can see the titles (copyright 1975).

Too many companies draft a policy, feel a smug sense of accomplishment, and then stash it in a drawer where it is never seen again, much less applied or even remembered. GDPR expects more than that.

Your internal company policies should set out the data protection rules of behavior for employees.

Policies are there to tell employees what the rules are but also to counsel and advise employees on how to carry out their jobs. Try and empathize with your employees when you are drafting them.

Why do we have to change our policies?

Maybe you don't. But GDPR has changed the rules on how you can process data and it is likely that your policies will need to be updated as a result.

What policies do we need to have in place to be GDPR compliant?

Part of the Accountability Principle under Article 5 of GDPR means you are expected to put in place appropriate corporate governance around personal data. Having appropriate policies in place is a big part of that corporate governance.

The essential policies are:

1.   Data Protection Policy

What is it? An essential guide to employees regarding how they may use data, how they can keep it secure, and the consequences of misuse.

Why do we need it? Employees cause many data breaches, and a good Data Protection Policy can prevent such breaches by helping employees understand how they are supposed to handle data.

2.   Data Retention Policy

What is it? A statement explaining when data in documents or held electronically should be destroyed or deleted. It sets out the time limits for deleting different types of documents.

Why do we need it? GDPR says that data cannot be kept for longer than necessary. Breaching this principle can attract the upper-tier of fines so we have to educate employees on data deletion.

3.   Data Breach Incident Policy

What is it? An emergency plan that tells your company what to do if a data breach occurs, how to form a team to deal with the breach, how to prevent any further loss of data and whether to tell customers and Regulators.

Why do we need it? So that vital time isn't wasted figuring out what to do if a disaster strikes. You want to protect your customer data and your job if you suffer a data breach. This is a critical policy.

What other policies should we consider putting into place?

There are a number of other Data Protection Policies that you should consider putting into place including:

- **Big Data Policy** – What you can and cannot do with Big Data under GDPR.
- **Human Resources and Data Protection Policy** – How to treat employee data.
- **Marketing and Data Protection Policy** – The rulebook on sending customers offers and promotions.
- **Social Media Policy** – Explains what employees are allowed to post on social media, sometimes including on private accounts.
- **Encryption Policy** – How, when and why we encrypt data.
- **Outsourcing Policy** – What you need to do if you are sending data to a business partner.
- **Bring Your Own Device Policy** – The manual on how to use a personal device in the course of your job.

Of course, some of the policies mentioned above can be rolled into your Data Protection Policy, but frequently it is more useful to have separate policies. Having one tome that covers all topics can be off-putting to employees. It is more manageable to split them into shorter policies on distinct topics.

Tips for your Data Protection Policies:

1.   **Make sure they are easy to find** - If a 22- year-old call center worker has a query about data protection from a customer, he should be able to access the Data Protection Policy at the click of a mouse for more details. I suggest putting the policies front and center on your intranet home page.

2.   **Mind your language** – Those dusty old policies have given way to easy-to-read documents written in plain English to be understood by regular people. There is no use drafting company policies for the members of the Board. Draft policies so that they will be understood by everyone from the Board to the most junior members of staff.

3.   **Keep them short** – Enough said.

4. **Be consistent** – Use the same introduction, sign off, and layout for all your company policies. Use an attractive layout.

5. **Don't be afraid to enforce your policy** – Proper Data Protection Governance is a much more important for companies post-GDPR. This means that companies have much more to lose if employees misbehave with customer data. Do not be afraid to discipline an employee if they have breached the Data Protection Policy.

Careless & Co. Co.'s Policies

As part of Careless & Co.'s marketing efforts, they collect customer data from many sources and use it to understand how to best send pop-up ads and marketing emails to customers who are likely to request the most loan money. Roger Ballentine decided to implement the following policies:

_X_ Data Protection Policy
___ Data Retention Policy
_X_ Data Breach Incident Policy
___ Big Data Policy
___ Human Resources and Data Protection Policy
_X_ Marketing and Data Protection Policy
___ Social Media Policy
_X_ Encryption Policy
___ Outsourcing Policy
_X_ Bring Your Own Device Policy

Careless & Co. knew it needed a Data Protection Policy, which also contained information on its policy on data retention. Careless created a Data Breach Incident Policy and a Rapid Response Team. It also decided to implement an Encryption Policy and Bring Your Own Device Policy.

Careless & Co. doesn't have a social media presence, nor is it particularly concerned about its employees' use of social media, so it decided to have a general statement in its Code of Conduct about not defaming the company. It also doesn't have outsourced services. It's Human Resources policies cover data protection, so they decided against a separate policy for this. Lastly, as Careless & Co. doesn't currently use Big Data analytics, it decided it doesn't need a policy for this.

Now It's Your Turn

Using the information gathered in Steps 1-4, determine which polices your organization needs to put in place. Beneath each policy, write out one to three key topics to cover for your company's specific data uses:

___ Data Protection Policy

_____
_____
_____
_____
_____
_____

__ Data Retention Policy

_____
_____
_____
_____
_____
_____

__ Data Breach Incident Policy

_____
_____
_____
_____
_____
_____
_____

__ Big Data Policy

_____
_____
_____
_____
_____
_____
_____

__ Human Resources and Data Protection Policy

_____
_____
_____
_____
_____
_____

__ Marketing and Data Protection Policy

_____
_____
_____
_____
_____
_____

__ Social Media Policy

_____
_____
_____
_____
_____
_____
_____

__ Encryption Policy

_____
_____
_____
_____
_____
_____
_____

__ Outsourcing Policy

_____
_____
_____
_____
_____
_____
_____

__ Bring Your Own Device Policy

_____
_____
_____
_____
_____
_____

Key Points:

- Most companies will need to change some policies to align with GDPR.
- You may need some new Data Protection Policies such as Data Breach Incident Plan, Big Data Policy, Human Resources and Data Protection Policy, Marketing and Data Protection Policy, Social Media Policy, and Bring Your Own Device Policy.
- Make sure your policies are:
    - Easy to find
    - Easy to understand
    - Short
    - Consistent
    - Enforced

Now that our policies are in place, let's get on the training train.

Notes on Implementation

STEP 7

Get on the Training Train

CONGRATULATIONS! YOU'VE COMPLETED YOUR Data Audit, made your Data Map, fixed your information security issues, and put in place your Privacy Notice(s) and Privacy Policies. You may have noticed most of this work was performed sitting at your desk. How will the average employee know about all the great work you've done? You have to get out there and spread the word about the changes you have made. You need to fire up the training train.

Why do we train staff on Data Protection and GDPR?

Staff training is one of the most crucial parts of GDPR. Your company staff will be processing data in all sorts of ways, and they need to know how to do it compliantly.

If you want them to process data according to your policies, you are going to need to make sure they have proper training on Data Protection and that includes GDPR.

Staff training on data security is critical to keeping data safe and avoiding the penalties of GDPR. One recent study said that human error is the leading cause of data breaches, featuring in 37% of data breaches.[7] You don't want your company to become a statistic.

Examples of data breaches that have been caused by employees include:

- A con man pretending to be the company CEO tricked an employee into sending the personal details of 700 staff members out of the company.
- A nurse's laptop containing sensitive unencrypted data was stolen.
- A lawyer stored sensitive case files on the family computer. The files were accidentally uploaded onto the Internet.
- An employee took a sensitive social worker's file and left it in his car. The car was then stolen.

How do we train staff?

Training is usually performed online and/or in person. Sometimes webinars take the place of in-person training, but feature a live person who can answer questions. Training can provide all staff with a working knowledge of Data Protection.

Online training

Many companies prefer to use online training courses because employees can individually choose the best time to take the course. Online training also provides a one-stop-shop for training, which can easily be deployed at a convenient time. For instance, if your company has employees on sick leave or parental leave, it is highly convenient to assign them the same course everyone else has taken when they return to work.

Online training can be procured in two ways: off-the-shelf and bespoke.

Off-the-Shelf Online Training

Many training companies have off-the-shelf training courses that can be taken by your employees online or loaded into your company's Learning Management System. It is generally more cost effective to buy an off-the-shelf version of online training. However, off-the-shelf courses are not tailored to the specific needs of your business.

Let's say that an off-the-shelf training course features a manufacturing environment in the example scenarios. If you are working at a technology company, it may be difficult for your employees to apply the lessons presented in the off-the-shelf training to their day-to-day activities.

Additionally, off-the-shelf training may not provide the specificity needed to teach employees in different roles about concepts that apply to their work. For example, Peter and Sumit work in a huge car repair company. Peter works in the call center and Sumit is in charge of the company's social media marketing. Peter and Sumit have very different privacy training needs because Peter needs trained on how to interact on the phone with customers whereas Sumit needs to be taught about privacy rules relating to marketing.

Lastly, employees may not take off-the-shelf training as seriously as bespoke training, because the training is typically not branded to your company. Some off-the-shelf products allow for customization, including adding a company's logo and a recorded message from the CEO. But it will be obvious to employees that the content of the course is not developed strictly for them.

Bespoke Online Training

Large companies or companies with highly creative, technologically skilled staff may choose to create their own online training courses. Some bespoke online training courses are created entirely in-house, while others are created in tandem with an outside vendor that develops such courses. Either way, a bespoke course is created entirely with your company and your policies in mind.

Developing a bespoke course takes time – usually between two and four months. However, once your company has the course, it should be able to deploy it for at least a year. If it is an introductory course, it may be assigned to all new employees for many years to come, making the investment more palatable. Perhaps the best part of bespoke online training is the ability to customize the course so it only touches on issues and scenarios your employees will face in the delivery of your product or services. This customization allows for better comprehension of the application of the law to the issues faced within your company.

Face-to-face training

In-person training can be highly successful if it is performed correctly. Most people are more engaged with a human than a computer screen, and a human can answer questions in real time, whereas a person watching the computer-based training has to write an email to get questions answered.

Face-to-face or webinar training needs to be structured appropriately for maximum engagement. Trainers must resist the impulse to be legalistic and to read a set of bullet point rules or to quote the GDPR in detail. Training should focus on the learner and what the learner needs to know to do his or her job properly and in accordance with the principles of the GDPR.

Face-to-face training may be prohibitively expensive if your company has offices in multiple states or countries. Some companies record live training, then push out the video to the company on its intranet or Learning Management System. Others invest in sending the trainer to multiple officers or countries, or have one set of PowerPoint slides delivered by different people in each office using a "Train-the-Trainer" model. "Train-the-Trainer" works when the creator or deliverer of the training goes through the slides with the other people who will be delivering the training and teaches them how to do it properly.

What do staff need to know about GDPR?

Regardless of whether you choose online training or the in-person model, determining what the staff needs to know is a crucial next step. Training needs may vary. What each person needs to know depends on the role that your various members of staff play. It is good for all staff to have a working knowledge of Data Protection issues generally.

General-employee training will usually include:

- A brief explanation of the law and why it is necessary to protect privacy;
- A description of the fines and reputational damage that can occur if the company does not comply;
- An explanation of the primary principles of the GDPR and how they apply to the activities of the company;
- Information on the main points of your company's Data Protection Policy and where it can be found;
- Information on where to get answers to questions.

Remember that people absorb training when they understand two things: (1.) Why the training is important to them and (2.) What they need to do in response to the training. You should be absolutely certain that your training includes this information, or people won't incorporate the training into their work.

Role-Specific Training

Some staff will need specialty knowledge on the different areas of GDPR. For example:

- **Call Center/Customer-Facing Staff** – Your call center staff will need a working knowledge of the Right to Erasure and the Right to Data Portability because customers may ask to assert these rights and there are strict time limits required for response.
- **Marketing Team** – Your marketeers will need to understand the new rules on consent.
- **Data Analytics Teams** – If you have any employees that are carrying out Big Data analytics then they will have to understand the new rules on profiling.

- **Senior Management** – It is important that senior management in areas such as Human Resources, Legal, and Sales are given solid training on how GDPR affects their areas so that they may cascade this knowledge down.
- **Human Resources** - The Human Resources team will need training on how to handle employee data including subject access requests and handling job application data.
- **Board** – You should advise the Board about the new fines under GDPR.

Avoid my mistakes!

I remember giving a training session to marketing staff early in my career as a Data Protection Officer. It was a three-hour session on Data Protection. I had over-prepared and came armed with slides bursting with legal information. The staff was looking forward to it about as much as one looks forward to root canal treatment. My marathon training session was only marginally less painful. I started to get an inkling of how badly I was going down when one guy started reading the writing on the back of his watch. I had failed to make my training engaging enough. Humbling? Absolutely. But afterwards I made a big effort to improve my future sessions by making them snappy, engaging, and discussing examples with the employees.

Top tips on making training engaging:

1.   **Keep it short** – Try and keep individual sessions to one hour or less. If you are doing half day training then make sure you give the staff plenty of breaks and exercises to do in groups or on their own. Being lectured to will not engage an audience for long. This is Data Protection after all.

2.   **Mirror your audience** – Find out who your audience is beforehand. If it is a room of 22-year-old sales employees, then you will want to use language and examples that appeal to them. Similarly, a presentation to the Board will require a more formal tone.

3.   **Make it practical** – The worst training session I ever sat through was one where the speaker just read out legal cases that related to the Eight Data Protection Principles. I will never get that day back. Don't make the same mistake. Make sure you give your staff examples of how GDPR applies to them.

For example, show your Marketing team examples of good and bad attempts to obtain customer consent. Then you can ask them to work through a series of example cases in groups, or put a scenario on your slides and ask them to talk it through with you leading the discussion. By making training as interactive as possible, you are much more likely to engage your audience.

Another example – let's say you're training your sales team. You might show them an example of how to deal with a customer who has sent an email requesting that his data be deleted. Perhaps you next ask them what they'd do with someone who says they want information on another client or customer's service, which might involve personal data. What should they do? Allow them to answer.

The Company Training Matrix

Once you've determined the type of training you will provide, the next step is to separate employees by category to determine where specialized training is needed, in addition to the general training. To do this, use the Company Training Matrix. The Company Training Matrix included three separate sections: (1.) Roles/Title(s), (2.) Type of Training and (3.) Subjects.

Careless & Co.

Careless & Co. has finished Steps 1-5. Roger's attention now turns to training. Who does he need to train and on what topics? Careless & Co. is a small company, so it has decided to do face-to-face training. It has a limited number of staff so it can easily deliver training in person.

The next step for Careless & Co. is to separate its employees by category to determine where specialized training is needed in addition to the general training. Careless & Co. filled in the Company Training Matrix as follows.

Role / Title(s)	Type of Training	Subjects
Sales, Admin, Brokers, Managers	General	Explanation of the GDPR Why it matters Explanation of policies Reporting / Data Breach Further Resources / Q&A
Human Resources	General plus Specialized	(Same General Training as above) Employee record-keeping Rights of employees under GDPR
Legal, Compliance, Information Technology, Information Security	General plus Specialized	(Same as General Training as above) International data transfer Privacy by Design Privacy Impact Assessments Obligations of Data Controllers and Processors
Board	General plus Specialized	(Same General Training as above) Fines International element of GDPR Role of the DPO in advising the Board New customer rights

Now It's Your Turn

Fill out the following Company Training Matrix for your organization.

Role / Title(s)	Type of Training	Subjects

Personalizing the Training

Now that you've determined your topics, think about examples you can add to your training for the different audiences. You can usually use the same slides for all presentations, but have different examples ready for each audience to make it as personal as possible.

Record, Record, Record

Just because you've done the training doesn't mean your work is done. If you don't keep proper training records, it's almost as if you didn't do the work.

Remember that Section A5(2) of GDPR says we have to "demonstrate compliance" with GDPR. In practice, this means you must keep good records of all training sessions delivered to staff.

Make sure that records of the time and date of training are kept in a safe place, both for online and face-to-face training. For online courses, most Learning Management Systems or training providers can produce reports to make your record keeping easy. Face-to-face training records can be made simply with a sign-in sheet at the door. Make a PDF of the sign-in sheet when the training is complete or add the names into an Excel sheet so you have an electronic record.

The Training Record Table can look like this:

Title of session and description of topics	Date	Trainer	Location	Duration	Attendees	Location of slides from session

Should a Regulator ever investigate your company, these records will be invaluable for proving your program's mettle.

Committing to proper record keeping can feel overwhelming when you're putting out fires within your company, but documentation can save the day if you're ever investigated. Proper documentation also allows you to show your Board, C-suite or management what you've been doing and to hold employees responsible for what they should be doing.

Key Points:

- Deliver basic data protection training that includes GDPR to all staff.
- Work out who needs face-to-face training.
- Make it engaging!
- Record all training you carry out.

Now that everyone knows what they're supposed to do on training, let's go on and assess the impact of future projects with Privacy Impact Assessments.

Notes on Implementation

_____

_____

_____

_____

_____

_____

_____

_____

_____

_____

_____

_____

_____

_____

_____

_____

STEP 8

Measuring the Impact with PIAs

THERE ARE MANY UNITS of measurement in the world. Seconds, ounces, pounds, kilograms, milligrams, degrees Fahrenheit, light years, the level of attractiveness of a potential partner … The list goes on and on. People love to measure things. It gives us context for our lives and helps us to compare one thing to another.

In the world of data privacy, we measure impact. Companies and practitioners need to know how much their initiatives are going to impact the privacy of the data subject.

What is a PIA?

A Data Privacy Impact Assessment ("PIA" sometimes called a "DPIA") is a risk assessment that a company should complete at the start of a new project if that project involves any material processing of customer data. PIAs usually take the form of a written document that is completed by the person in charge of the project and signed off by a person in authority.

The DPO in a company will usually be the person who is drafting and sending out PIAs. Under GDPR, companies must seek the advice of their DPO (if they have one) when completing the PIA.

The point of the PIA is to:

- Detail potential privacy risks of the project;
- List the ways in which those risks can be reduced;
- Have the risks signed off by the appropriate person within the company;
- Ensure the situation is monitored so that recommendations are carried out.

Implementing a PIA process will help you understand the potential data privacy problems that exist at an early stage so you can fix them and stay on the right side of the law.

Why do I hear so much talk about PIAs now?

There are new responsibilities under GDPR around assessing the privacy risk for new projects.

Under Article 35 of GDPR, controllers must do an assessment of the privacy risk on a project where *"it is likely to result in a high risk to the rights and freedoms"* of individuals. You can also complete a PIA voluntarily even when you are not obliged to under GDPR. This can be useful to show Regulators if they ever investigate your processes.

The fact that we have to "demonstrate compliance" under Article 5 of GDPR is important too, because PIAs are evidence that a company takes data privacy seriously. And this evidence can be useful if a Regulator decides to pay you a visit.

GDPR says we must complete a PIA when the project involves:

- Use of data for "profiling" such as monitoring customer behavior on your website so that you know which pop-up ads to send to particular customers when they are online;
- A large amount of sensitive (or "special categories" of data[8]) such as transferring all your customer medical records to a cloud provider;
- Monitoring a publicly accessible area on a large scale, such as capturing CCTV footage of a public park.

But PIAs are not limited to the examples listed above. We must complete a PIA for any data project that poses a "high risk" to the privacy rights and freedoms of individuals.

At what stage should a PIA be carried out?

A PIA should be carried out at the start of a project so that the people involved in the project can be informed of any privacy risks. Solutions to these risks can then be built into the project at the earliest possible stage.

If you hear of a project that has started without a completed PIA, then you should ask for the PIA to be completed a PIA as soon as possible.

What are the sections of a PIA?

Many of the PIAs I have seen have been overly complicated. PIAs should be simple and clear.

Your PIA template form may cover the following areas. Some of these areas are legal requirements, as noted:

- **Initial questions to see if a PIA is needed.** These include questions such as "Does the project use data?" or "Does the project use data in a new way?"
- **Briefly explain what the project is about.** You want the project owner to fill out this section. For example, the project owner may write: "This is a project by the Big Data team to analyze customer's financial information from last year."
- **Describe the type of data involved.** For example, "The customer's name and most recent account balance."
- **Describe how the data is used.** For example, "Customer data will be used to see which customers will be most likely to buy mortgage products." This is a legal requirement under GDPR.
- **Identify the lawful basis** or legitimizing condition being relied upon under GDPR for processing the data. For example, "We have the customer's consent."
- **Identify the privacy risks**. For example, "Security risks exist while moving the data from one department to another during the project." This is a legal requirement.
- **Identify solutions** to the privacy risks/risk management. For example, "Check that all consents are current and valid." This is a legal requirement.

- **Necessary and Proportionate?** You are required to consider whether the data used in a project is necessary and proportionate. You should ask, "Do we need to do this?" This consideration is a legal requirement for the PIA process.
- **Recommendations from the DPO** – The DPO should review the PIA and make recommendation on topics such as data security and consent.
- **Sign off on the risk from the person in charge** – It is important that the Senior Member of the project has been made aware of the risks and has agreed to them in writing. The Board may need to be aware of the project as well as the Head of Compliance if the privacy risks are significant.

Example PIA

Here's a short PIA example that you can use with your company:

Name of Person Completing PIA	
Contact Information for Project Manager	
Does the Project use personal data?	
Briefly explain the project	
What kinds of personal data are involved? (e.g., email addresses, phone numbers etc.)	
How will this personal data be used?	
What is the lawful basis for using this data? (You may need to contact the Data Protection Officer to answer this question)	
Is the data use in project necessary and proportionate?	
What privacy risks are involved in this project?	
What solutions should be implemented to mitigate these privacy risks?	

What recommendations has the Data Privacy Officer given to mitigate risk for this project?	
Signature of the person in charge of the project	

Top Tips on PIAs:

Keep them concise. Draft a simple, jargon-free document that is no more than three pages long. This ensures that the projects team is likely to use the document.

Explain the document.

George Bernard Shaw famously said, "The single biggest problem in communication is that it has taken place."

To communicate the PIA, you must get out into your company to tell them about the merits of your new PIA process.

Emailing the document en masse is not enough. Organize a few meetings to show the PIA to various teams.

Make sure the entire company knows about your PIA forms and how to complete them. PIAs are not just for project teams. Many departments of your company will be involved in processing data in different ways. You should ensure the entire company knows about the PIA form so it will be properly used.

Following are three examples of when a PIA should be completed:

- The Marketing Department may decide to send text messages to 500 customers to tell them about new offers.
- Building Security may decide to install CCTV to monitor activity on the street near the building.
- The Legal Department may wish to contract with a Cloud provider in Japan.

Who should sign off your PIA?

Someone sufficiently senior who has the authority to approve risks relating to the project should sign off on the PIA. The DPO will advise and recommend how to mitigate the risk of data within a project but he should not sign it off on it. Under Article 39 of GDPR, it is the DPO's job to "inform and advise" on Data Protection. The business must make the ultimate decision about whether to go forward with each project and which mitigating controls they wish to put in place.

The DPO can advise on the extent of the risk (i.e. she can tell the company whether the risks are small, medium or a large) and she can advise whether she thinks the project should go ahead or not. But it is not her job to decide whether to actually assume the risk. This belongs to whoever has that authority within your company to approve the project.

Careless & Co.

The Marketing team at Careless & Co. has decided they want to move their customer database to a new cloud provider called Fluffy Storage, which offers less expensive storage solutions than their current provider. Roger sends the PIA to Aliana, the Head of Marketing. She completes it as follows:

Name of Person Completing PIA	Aliana Huff
Contact Information for Project Manager	Aliana.Huff@carelessandco.com
Does the Project use personal data?	Yes
Briefly explain the project	We want to move our customer database to a new cloud provider called Fluffy Storage.
What kinds of personal data are involved? (e.g., email addresses, phone numbers etc.)	Customer names, addresses, and phone numbers as well as credit check information.
How will this personal data be used?	It will be used to house the information of previous customers who have not applied for a new loan in the previous 12 months.
What is the lawful basis for using this data? (You may need to contact the Data Protection Officer to answer this question)	It is in our legitimate interest to do this.
Is the data use in this project necessary and proportionate?	Yes, and it is reasonable for us to change to this new cloud provider.
What privacy risks are involved in this project?	Security risk in transferring large amount of data to a third party cloud provider.
What solutions should be implemented to mitigate these privacy risks?	Ensure that data as minimized i.e. we are not sending more than we need to Fluffy. Ensure data is encrypted when it is in transit to Fluffy.
What recommendations has the Data Privacy Officer given to mitigate risk for this project?	Get proper contract clauses in place between us and Fluffy (see Step 9). Do not send more to them more data than we have to. Get them to agree to encrypt data in transit. Keep an eye on Fluffy to make sure they are behaving properly throughout the contract.
Signature of the person in charge of the project	*Aliana Huff*

When the form is complete, Roger sends it to the CEO and the other senior managers in the company to see whether they want to proceed with the project or not.

PIAs Tracker Sheet

In order to stay on top of your PIAs, you should have one spreadsheet or PIA Tracker that contains details of all of your PIAs. PIA Trackers should contain the following information:

PIA Number	Notified by	Date received	Current status: Pending/ completed	Summary of issues	Risk signed off by and date	Summary of advice given by DPO and date

Who is in charge of making sure that the recommendations are carried out?

If there is a DPO in your company, under Article 39 the DPO must "monitor compliance." The DPO must ensure the recommendations in the PIA are carried out.

If there is no DPO in your company, it is less clear who should be ensuring the recommendations are carried out. It is risky to have a PIA with recommendations that are not carried out because your company will not have "demonstrated compliance" with GDPR as it is obliged to under Article 5.

Write up your PIA afterwards

After the PIA is completed and signed off, you should write up a summary of the privacy-related risks and then circulate the summary to the people who should know about them. If the PIA relates to a risky project, make sure the people at the highest echelons of your company know about it.

Is that the end?

Unfortunately not. Projects can be complex, and they can take many twists and turns. Often there is "function creep" in projects where it is begun with good intentions on data, but after a while controls become weaker. This is why the DPO needs to keep a close eye on the project.

It is important for you to monitor projects to ensure that any requirements that were agreed upon in the PIA are being carried out. Remember to record any evidence you have gathered that shows compliance with the PIA.

Example: Junk4Cash

Let's take another example of the PIA process. The Board at Junk4Cash, a junk-hauling firm, has directed the company to install a closed-caption television system (CCTV) outside its building for security purposes. Melanie has been put in charge of procuring the CCTV provider. She opens the PIA form and works with Augustus, Junk4Cash's Co.'s DPO, to complete it.

Melanie noted in the PIA that there were several privacy concerns, including the need to notify people they might be recorded on the video feed from the CCTV. Augustus made the following recommendations based on Melanie's PIA:

- Put up a notice advising people CCTV cameras are present;
- Delete footage after three days unless it was needed to investigate a crime;
- Ensure that camera points at the entrance of the building and not past the entrance onto the street;
- Make sure the access to the footage is limited to those employees who need to see it; and
- Make sure the footage is stored on a secure server and encrypt the footage if it is being transferred.

Melanie read Augustus' recommendations and committed to following them. A month later, Augustus followed up to ensure the recommendations were implemented. He then updated the PIA to close it out. He took a picture of the notice advising people that CCTV cameras were present and linked the PIA to the procedures document that showed that CCTV footage was deleted after three days. He also took a picture of the footage from the CCTV control room showing that the camera only recorded footage of the building entrance and not the street.

What happens when you have advised a business not to carry out a certain project but they want to proceed anyway?

If the business wants to proceed on a project after having been advised against it, it is crucial the advice is recorded and the risk is communicated to the right people within your company.

For example, let's say the Marketing Department in a retailer called Jeans Star wants to buy data from a Lead Generation Company called MarketBoyz. Selena, Jeans Star's DPO, has serious concerns. She is worried the consent MarketBoyz's customers originally gave to MarketBoyz does not allow MarketBoyz to sell the data to Jeans Star. The situation is not cut and dried but Selena is not completely satisfied that the consents are adequate. She advises against the project on the PIA form, but the business decides to proceed anyway. She takes the following steps:

1. She tells the Marketing Department about the potential consequences.
2. She tells others within Jean Star – She advises the Head of Compliance, the Head of Risk and the Head of Legal about the situation. She also informs the Board of Directors so everyone can be fully informed of the magnitude of this risk.
3. She makes sure the CEO who is signing off on the project is aware of the risks, including the GDPR fines.
4. She records everything – Selena records the advice she gave saying the project should not go ahead and keeps it in a safe place.
5. She keeps a close eye – Selena keeps a close eye on the project to make sure any recommendations made to reduce the risk are carried out.

Key Points:

- PIAs are a fundamental part of GDPR and it is a breach of GDPR not to use them for "high risk" data projects.
- PIAs should cover risks, recommendations, solutions, and sign off.
- Keep PIAs concise, and explain the document to your company.
- Have a PIA tracker to stay on top of your PIAs.
- Keep an eye on the projects.
- Be careful if the business wants to proceed despite having been told of serious risks.

Now that we've implemented our PIA process, let's move on from the world of managing data to the murky world of preparing for and reporting data breaches.

Notes on Implementation

What to Do When It All Goes Wrong: Preparing for and Reporting Data Breaches

IF YOU'RE IN CHARGE of data protection, at some point you'll probably wake up to a frantic call or a panicked email telling you there's been a data breach. If you're in a large organization, this may be a weekly event. Data breaches vary dramatically in size, from an attachment containing personal data being emailed to the wrong individual, to a full-scale ransomware attack that holds the company hostage.

Being prepared for the inevitable data breach makes them much easier to manage. Notification requirements under the GDPR have tightened dramatically compared to previous requirements, so it pays to be prepared.

This section will help you to comply with the breach notification requirements of the GDPR, but if your data breach involves citizens of countries outside the EU, you should work with the Legal Department or outside counsel to ensure you're following the breach notification requirements of other countries.

What's the story?

Under Article 33 of GDPR there is a legal obligation for companies to report significant data breaches (breaches) to the Regulator. Companies must also report certain breaches to individuals affected by a breach – this is set out in Article 34.

The maximum fine for not reporting a significant breach is up to €10m or 2% of global annual turnover, sums that could give your Board sleepless nights!

The Data Breach Response Plan.

Suffering a data breach is inevitable for most companies.

Your company is going to need a Data Breach Response Plan (Plan) in place so it knows how to respond to a cyberattack or any other type of data breach.

Keep the Plan short and simple – The last thing you need in the middle of a Data Breach is for people to be running around trying to figure out what the plan means. Don't over engineer it.

Create a Rapid Response Team

A Rapid Response team is a group of people who are pre-chosen and trained to deal with a data breach. Creating a Rapid Response team is a critical part of data breach preparation.

Rapid Response teams typically include named individuals from IT Security, Compliance, Human Resources, Marketing, and Legal. Depending on your company's structure, you may want to include someone from Communications, Public Relations, and/or the business.

Document the membership of the Rapid Response team within your Plan. Make sure everyone on the Rapid Response team's contact information (including mobile phone number) is included in the Plan. Set out the responsibilities of each team member in the document, and make sure all members of the team know what they should do. For example, Legal may need to review contracts to determine whether the customer should be notified, while Compliance may be assigned breach notification research. Communications or Public Relations might be tasked with drafting holding statements or communications to the media regarding the breach.

Practice runs should be performed so the team knows how to operate in the event of a real breach.

Careless and Co.

Roger Ballentine was excited to create Careless & Co.'s first Rapid Response Team. He always enjoyed pro-actively working on prevention, rather than responding to problems. He put together his Rapid Response Team as follows.

Company Department	Should they be involved (Yes/No)?	Tasks Assigned
Legal	Yes	Review contracts to see if there are data breach terms Advise on any legal issues that crop up during a breach
Communications	Yes	Draft customer-facing statements for those worried about the breach Draft media-facing statements (proactive and reactive if required)
Compliance	Yes	Decide whether to notify Regulators of breach, draft notice(s) to same Decide whether to notify data subjects of breach, draft notice(s) to same

Company Department	Should they be involved (Yes/No)?	Tasks Assigned
Finance	No	
IT Security	Yes	In charge of stopping breach and planning remediation of controls so it doesn't happen again
Internal Audit	No	
Board of Directors	No	
Human Resources	No	
Sales/Business Managers	Yes	Business will lead communications with client about breach since they have the relationship
Operations	No	

Now it's Your Turn

Begin creating your Rapid Response Team here. Decide whether it makes sense for each of the following functions to be part of your Rapid Response team, and consider which tasks should be assigned to each.

Company Department	Should they be involved (Yes/No)?	Tasks Assigned
Legal		
Communications		
Compliance		
Finance		
IT Security		
Internal Audit		
Board of Directors		
Human Resources		
Sales/Business Managers		
Operations		

What else should I include in my Plan?

- **Information on containing the breach** – Your Plan should include tips for containing breaches as soon as they occur so that you can limit the damage.

- **Contact information for a third-party IT Team on standby** – A team trained in crisis management and incident response should be able to help you deal with the immediate aftermath of the breach. Find these professionals before you need them and either put them on retainer or have them on speed-dial.
- **Template Internal Breach Report** – Draft a template report and have it ready to complete when an incident occurs. The finalized report should include information on what happened and how to prevent it happening again. It should also contain details of any improvements that must be added to the company's systems and controls.
- **Checklist of Records** – Prepare a checklist that will tell the company which records to keep so you can prove all of the steps you took to manage the breach.
- **Flow-chart for Reporting** – Create a flowchart detailing when to report the breach to the employees, Regulators or customers.

When it All Goes Wrong – Reporting a Data Breach

When a data breach occurs, the first question after, "Is it contained?" is "Who, if anyone, do we have to notify?" Notification can be painful, but with some pre-planning, it can be easier to manage.

What do I need to know about notifying the Regulator of a Data Breach?

You, as a Controller, have to notify the Regulator of a breach if the breach is likely to result in "a risk to the rights and freedoms of individuals." Like so much of GDPR, this is a judgment call as to when a data breach meets this threshold.

For example, if there is a breach and a hacker steals 20 customers' credit card details, this would undoubtedly qualify as a breach that should be reported to the Regulator because it represents a risk to the rights and freedoms of individuals.

However, if there is a breach where a document containing only the names of 30 customers who entered a competition to win a weekend in New York were lost on the street, then it is unlikely that this would need to be reported to the Regulator.

If you need to report a breach to the Regulator, notice must be made within 72 hours of the company becoming aware of the breach.

What should I include in my breach report to the Regulator?

There are certain pieces of information you'll need to report to the Regulator. Article 33 of GDPR says you have to include specifics, including:

- Details about the number of people and records involved.
- The categories of personal data involved.
- Name of the DPO or other contact within the company.
- Description of the likely consequences of the breach.
- A description of how you intend to deal with the breach.

Pre-Drafting Makes It Easier

In the heat of a data breach that is impactful enough to need to be reported to the Regulator, people tend to be so panicked they aren't thinking straight. It can very helpful to have a draft email or letter to the Regulator so you can simply fill in the information. Here's an example:

Dear [Regulator],

By way of this communication, [Company name] is reporting a data breach involving [number of people / records involved] that occurred on [date of incident or dates of incident in the case of a breach that went on for some time]. The categories of personal data involved in this data breach are [insert categories of data involved].

[Name of Data Protection Officer] is the Data Protection Officer for our company. S/he can be contacted at [insert email address and phone number for Data Protection Officer.

Because of this breach, [describe the likely consequences of the breach]. We intend to mitigate the damages caused by this breach by [explain how you're going to deal with it].

Sincerely,

[Name of reporting person]

Do I also have to tell the affected people about a Data Breach?

Maybe. If your company suffers a data breach that results in a "high risk to the rights and freedoms" of customers/individuals (I will use "customers" for ease of reference), you will have to tell the customers about the breach. This appears at Article 34 of GDPR.

For example, if a customer's financial records are hacked at a bank, the customer could suffer financial loss through identity theft or fraud due to the records being accessed. The customer needs to be told about this.

If you have to report a breach to the customer, GDPR says the report must be made "*without undue delay.*"

Review the Contract

Please note many contracts include data breach notification requirements that may be stricter than the GDPR's. For example, some of your suppliers and business partners may require that all data breaches relating to data of their employees or customers be reported to them, even if the breach does not involve "high risk to the rights and freedoms" of those involved. Other contracts may require reporting to the supplier within 24 or 48 hours. Be sure to check contracts with your suppliers to make sure that you know what they want you to do if a data breach happens.

What should I include in my breach report to customers?

Section A34 of GDPR says you should tell the customer:

- The name of the DPO or other contact within the company.
- A description of the consequences of the breach.
- A description of how you intend to deal with the breach.

Make sure you explain the breach to the customer simply and clearly.

Once Again, Pre-Drafting Makes It Easier

Data breaches relating to customers and key clients can lead to meltdown for management and the Board. Having a pre-drafted outlined message can make the notification process simpler.

Dear [Customer Name],

We regret to inform you that on [date or dates] we experienced a [hacking/loss of data/ accidental loss /intentional attack/ or other type of breach]. Unfortunately, your [state categories of data] was [lost/stolen/potentially exposed / other things that happened to it]. We have [explain what has been done to cure the breach] and believe that [outcome – data is now secure / problem is solved].

Our Data Protection Officer's is [name of Data Protection Officer] and she can be reached at [email address and phone number]. [If further help is being offered – like credit tracking services, write that here. If not, erase this sentence]. Please note that there are some useful FAQs on our website at [enter web address] about this [hacking/loss of data/ accidental loss /intentional attack/ or other type of breach] and we also have a helpline at [enter phone number] should you have any queries.

Please know that [name of company] takes data security extremely seriously, and we apologize for any inconvenience this may cause.

Sincerely,

[Company representatives]

What about when I am a Processor? Do I have to report a breach to anyone?

Under Article 33, the Processor has to notify the Controller without undue delay.

Three top tips you for efficient breach reporting:

1. **Employee Instructions**: If an employee finds out about a data breach, he or she must tell you about it quickly. Provide employees with an email address so that when they report a breach, the right people can act on it immediately. Include these details in the Data Protection Policy and train, train, train employees so they understand they must immediately report a breach to the DPO or an equivalent person in your company. Remember employees are your eyes and ears for breaches and you want to avoid the company being fined for not reporting a breach. They need to be aware of the time limits for reporting breaches also.

2. **Keeping Mum**: Make sure your employees know not to make statements to the media. And make sure your employees know that they are not allowed to talk about the breach on social media – especially if they are feeling tired and emotional. It is useful to have your Communications department send the employees an email explaining the breach and explaining what they can and cannot do in relation to the breach.

3. **Record**: Be sure to keep a record of what occurred and how the breach was handled. One way to do this is with a Data Breach Recording Template.

Keeping Records

Like everything else in data protection, you'll want to keep records of data breaches and how they were handled. This is especially important if the Regulator performs an investigation.

A Data Breach Recording Template might look like this:

No.	Incident summary	Personal Data involved including volume and categories	Name and email of DPO/person to be contacted within the company	Description of likely consequence of breach	How we intend to deal with the breach including whether regulators or customers will be informed

Careless & Co.

Careless & Co. did everything it could to keep its data secure. However, Alan, a senior manager in the Accounting Department, clicked on a link in an email that allowed a virus to infiltrate Careless & Co.'s network. As a result, an Excel spreadsheet was exposed. The spreadsheet included customer names, addresses, amounts of the loan, and reasons the loans were requested. Ten of the applications were for loans to cover medical bills or medical procedures.

Roger, Careless & Co.'s DPO, found out about the breach and immediately called a data security firm to ensure the virus was removed from the network and systems, and the firewall was strengthened.

Careless' Rapid Response team worked with outside counsel to determine that it needed to notify both the Data Protection Authority in the UK and the customers whose loan records contained health-related information. Careless reviewed the files that were accessed and found that all of the data subjects involved were citizens of the UK.

Next, Careless wrote an email to the Data Protection Authority. It read:

Dear Representative of the Information Commissioners' Office,

By way of this communication, Careless & Co. is reporting a data breach involving the records of 10 data subjects that occurred on March 15. The categories of personal data involved in this data breach are customer names, addresses, and health-related information including whether customers have applied for a loan for medical procedures or to pay medical bills.

Roger Ballentine is the Data Protection Officer for our company. He can be contacted at Rballentine@Carelessandco.com and phoned at +44 (0)22 2325 266.

Because of this breach, some information about medical procedures or bills may have been viewed or copied. We intend to mitigate the damages caused by this breach by notifying the affected data subjects by email. We have already taken steps to remove the virus from the systems and strengthened our firewalls. Please feel free to contact us if you have any questions.

Sincerely,

Sita Alessandro

Chief Compliance Counsel

Careless then sent the following email to all of the affected customers:

Dear Valued Member,

We regret to inform you that on March 15, our network was exposed to a virus attack. Unfortunately, your name, address and loan-related information (which may include health-related information about the reason you applied for the loan) were potentially accessed. We have expelled the virus from our systems and strengthened our firewall, and believe that the issue is now resolved.

Our Data Protection Officer is Roger Ballentine and he can be reached at Rballentine@carelessandco.com and phoned at +44 (0)22 2325 266. We have created an information line that you can call to find out if there was health-related information of yours in our records that may have been accessed. That number is ++44 (0)197 5225 253. Please note there are some useful FAQs on our website about this intentional attack at www.verycarelessdudes.com/FAQs. We also have a helpline at +44 (0)197 5225 253 should you have any queries.

Please know that Careless & Co. takes data security extremely seriously, and we apologize for any inconvenience this may cause.

Sincerely,

Sita Alessandro

Roger then filled out his Data Breach Recording Template as follows:

No.	Incident summary	Personal Data involved including volume and categories	Name and email of DPO/person to be contacted within the company	Description of likely consequence of breach	How we intend to deal with the breach including whether regulators or customers will be informed
1	A virus entered the network. It was caused by a manager clicking on a link within an email, which exposed the network to the virus.	Customer names, addresses, and loan-related information, which included health-related information. 10 records were compromised	Roger Ballentine, Rballentine@carelessandco.com	Notification was required and made to the Data Protection Authority and to customers whose records may have been accessed. The records of these letters are stored in the DPO folder.	We hired a specialist firm to ensure the virus was removed from the system and strengthened the firewall.

Now It's Your Turn

Pre-draft your Data Protection Regulator notification outline here:

_____
_____
_____
_____
_____
_____
_____
_____
_____
_____

_____
_____
_____
_____
_____
_____
_____
_____
_____
_____

Now Pre-draft your Data Subject notification outline here:

_____
_____
_____
_____
_____
_____
_____
_____
_____
_____
_____
_____
_____
_____
_____
_____
_____
_____
_____
_____

Key Points:

- Under GDPR, you have to notify the Regulator within 72 hours of a breach where it is likely to result in *"a risk to the rights and freedoms of individuals."*
- You must promptly notify customers about a data breach that results in a "high risk to their rights and freedoms."
- Make sure employees who learn of a Data Breach tell you about it immediately. This should be in your Data Protection Policy.
- Bad things happen sometimes – create a Data Breach Plan to guide your company in its response.

Now that you made it through data breach preparation, it's time to deal with your suppliers and third parties that have access to your organization's personal data.

Notes on Implementation

STEP 10

Dealing with Third Party Pain

WORKING WITH PERSONAL DATA can make you feel like a parent. You protect it, trying to make sure it is secure at all times. You provide the best place you can for it to live. But someday, it will have to go off on its own to other places. It will be out of your view and protection. Other people may not treat it as carefully as you do, or store it as well, or keep it safe in the same way.

While parents may need to let their kids grow up and leave home, your job in data protection is to manage what happens when other people or organizations get their hands on your data.

You may have wondered why there has been so much talk around the subject third parties. You may have thought if you keep your own house in order, you do not need to worry about what anyone else is doing with your data. Wrong.

No company is an island. In the globalized world in which we live, companies often have business partners scattered around the globe, some of which they have never met. From the guy who fills your vending machines to the real estate conglomerate from which you rent your offices, your company is likely to share data with many third parties.

Many third parties will need access to your customer data. Under GDPR, we have to be more careful than ever before to ensure we only hand over our customer data to business partners who will look after it.

When we decide to share data with a third party, we have to confirm we have put proper contractual clauses in place so that we are covered if they ever lose our data.

We'll look at two common scenarios in this Step. What to do when:

- You are acting as a Data Controller (or a "Controller" as the GDPR puts it) and sharing the data with Data Processors ("Processors"); and
- You are a Processor handling data on behalf of a Controller.

What is a Processor and what is a Controller?

Under Article 4 of GDPR, a "Controller" is the company that decides how the data is processed. A "Processor" is a company that processes the data on behalf of the Controller.

When companies do business and share data, is there always a Controller and a Processor in the relationship?

No. In some cases when parties share data, they may both have authority to over the data, and they may therefore both be Controllers. An example might be an insurance broker called CarSafe. CarSafe has a shop and sells car insurance to customers in Cookstown. CarSafe shares data with the underwriter called BigCo in London who provides the financial backing for the policies. Both CarSafe and BigCo are Controllers because neither is the servant of the other.

Why do I have to worry about suppliers and Data Security?

Often the Data Breaches, you hear about in the news are caused by a company's business partners or suppliers, rather than the company itself. The Target incident mentioned earlier in the book was a prime example. Forty million customer credit card details were compromised after hackers gained access via one of Target's third-party vendors.

What to do if you are a Controller doing business with a Processor

What do I need know about choosing a Processor?

Under GDPR, there are some very specific rules around choosing Processors. Specifically, under Article 28 you can only choose a Processor that provides "sufficient guarantees" that they will uphold GDPR. Remember this is the "show not tell" regulation, so you are going to need solid evidence the Processor you are doing business with is going to be able to keep the data safe and give you evidence they are able to do so.

This means that your company is going to have to do due diligence on any new supplier you do business with.

Top Tips for Due Diligence on Processors:

1. **Have an Outsourcing Policy on hiring new Processors** – Put a company policy in place detailing a procedure for hiring new Processors. The policy should set out the kind of homework required each time you hire a new Processor to make sure they are the type of organization you would trust with your customer data.

The policy could include steps such as requiring the return of a questionnaire providing details of the Processor's Data Security procedures. It could also include investigating the Processor's history and public profile to verify that they are trustworthy.

2. **Security standards** – Check to see if the Processor has obtained certification to any security-related standard, such as ISO 27001.

3. **Evidence** – Ask the potential Processor for evidence of their data security procedures. Don't take their word for it.

4. **Record** – Record all the due diligence you have carried out on the Processor.

Contracts – What do I have to do to make sure my contracts are up to par with GDPR?

Under GDPR, you have to make sure your Processors agree to a number of clauses regarding how they will use with your data. It is a breach of GDPR if your Processors do not sign up to these clauses.

Make sure that Legal or whoever drafts your supplier agreements includes the clauses that are listed at Article 28 of GDPR.

Under Article 28 if you are a Controller choosing a Processor, there has to be a contract in place saying the Processor:

- Will do as they are told with the data.
- Will only employ people who have promised to keep the data confidential.
- Will keep the data secure.
- Will not hire another Processor to do the work unless the Controller has given permission.
- Will help the Controller fulfill requests brought by customers enforcing their rights under GDPR. For example, if a customer puts in a request for her data to be wiped under the Right of Erasure, then the Processor will help the Controller by wiping any data off their (i.e. the Processor's) systems if the Controller asks them to.
- Will help the Controller with their GDPR duties including breach notification requirements. So, if the Processor loses some of the data given to it by the Controller, the Processor will tell the Controller so that the Controller will be able to report the breach to the Regulator within the 72-hour time limit.
- Will delete the data at the end of the contract.
- Will allow their processes to be inspected and audited.

Please check Article 28 to see these clauses in more detail.

Further tips for Controller contracts with Processors:

1. **Include a good indemnity clause** – Include a clause saying the Processor will reimburse you for all losses you sustain if ever there is a data breach involving your data.
2. **Cyber Insurance** – Make sure you see evidence of your Processor's cyber insurance policy. You need to know they can cover your losses if they ever drop the ball (See Step 4 – Keeping Your Data Secure for more details on what your cyber insurance policy should say).

Do I have to redraft all the contracts that were in force before GDPR?

No. No one expects you to trawl through and change every agreement you had in place before the GDPR came into force. However, there may be some higher-risk agreements you'll want to renegotiate with your suppliers.

For example, if a Processor handles large amount of your customer data, you may be concerned that there is inadequate protection for you in this agreement if things go wrong. You may want to consider contacting the Processor and renegotiating the contract to ensure compliance with GDPR.

Cloud Providers and Outsourced IT

Be extra careful when dealing with cloud providers. Cloud providers handle huge amounts of customer data and often store it in various parts of the globe. You should do your homework on the cloud provider before handing over terabytes of customer data. Similarly, ensure you have appropriate clauses in the contract to protect you if they lose your data.

Also, be careful if you are dealing with outsourced IT services. You should make sure the contract spells out the responsibilities the IT service provider has; such as updating software, monitoring data etc. A properly drafted contract will protect you if something goes wrong.

What to do if you are a Processor doing business with a Controller

Things to know if you are a Processor:

1. **You are in the frame now** – Under the old regime, the EU Data Protection law did not catch a Processor, and so even if they dropped the ball, Regulators could not fine them. Under GDPR, this has changed. Processors are now subject to GDPR. That means they can be fined or subject to action from the Regulator if they misbehave or lose data. Make sure your company knows there are increased risks when processing data on behalf of another company. Let your risk team know, let your board know, and let Legal know so they are aware it is more hazardous to be a Processor than it was before.

2. **Cyber Insurance** – You may have noticed I have a bit of an obsession with cyber insurance. This is because it is more important than ever to make sure your company has a safety net if ever there were an issue with data. Cyber insurance is important for Processors.

Let's say IceceCream is an ice cream company. They hire a company called Slick Call Centers Inc., which provides a customer service helpline to IceceCream customers. If Slick's systems fail and they lose IceceCream's customer data, Slick could be fined and end up with expensive problems that offering free ice cream isn't going to fix. Slick should get insurance in place to cover them if they face lawsuits from IceceCream customers and Regulator fines.

3. **Don't let the Controller take your trousers** – While there are contractual clauses that Controllers have to put into contracts with Processors, be vigilant about anything not required by GDPR. Controllers will try to make you liable for everything under the sun. If something goes wrong, they'll try to make you foot the bill. Make sure you do not agree to any unreasonably harsh clauses – and do not let Controllers take too much from you if there is a data breach. Otherwise you could be walking home with no trousers.

4. **Subprocessors** – If you as a Processor hire someone else to help you do what the Controller has asked you to do (a 'Subprocessor') then you need to sign to Subprocessor up to clauses a-h on page 102.

Careless & Co.

Careless & Co. was doing so well it decided it was time to outsource payroll at the company. For the longest time, the Finance Department ran payroll, but as that department was increasingly busy, and it became clear that moving to a full-time payroll provider was the best course of action.

Careless & Co. chose Super Pay Inc. as its payroll company. Careless & Co.'s Legal Department began drafting the contract with Super Pay. They asked Roger Ballentine what should be included in the contract. He told them to include the following:

- Evidence they would always hold insurance with at least a $1 million limit
- Indemnity in case of breach
- Obligations under GDPR Article 28, which include:
  - Super Pay can only do what Careless & Co. says with the data.
  - Super Pay will only use employees who have promised to keep the data confidential.
  - Super Pay will keep the data secure.
  - Super Pay will not hire another Processor without express permission from Careless & Co.

- Super Pay will help Careless to execute all of its customers' rights under GDPR.
- Super Pay will help the Careless Co. with its GDPR duties, including breach notification so Careless can report to the Regulator if necessary within seventy-two hours.
- Super Pay will delete the data at the end of the contract.
- Super Pay will allow their processes to be inspected and audited.

Now it's your turn

Choose a critical supplier contract you want to update for GDPR. Use the checklist below to determine which sections need to be updated or included in the contract:

- Evidence the Processor will always hold insurance with at least a $_____ limit
- Indemnity in case of breach
- Obligations under GDPR Article 28, which include:
  - They can only do what you say with the data
  - They only use employees who have promised to keep the data confidential
  - They will keep the data secure
  - They will not hire another Processor without you agreeing
  - They will help you with to execute all customer rights under GDPR
  - They will help you with you GDPR duties including breach notification
  - They will delete the data at the end of the contract
  - They will allow their processes to be inspected and audited.

Key Points:

- Suppliers often cause data breaches.
- GDPR expects you to choose suppliers wisely.
- Make sure your contracts contain all required GDPR clauses.
- If you are a Processor providing a service for a Controller, you have more risks now than you did before.
- Be careful with cloud providers and outsourced IT.

Congratulations! You've made it through all Ten Steps to GDPR Compliance. Think you're finished and you can sit back and relax? Maybe for a brief minute. But this quest continues...

Notes on Implementation

What Now? Record, Record, Record

IMAGINE HOW AWFUL IT would feel to be hauled in front of the Board of Directors or a Regulator if you haven't documented your program. "Training? Sure, we've done tons of it. I mean, I know we did. I assigned it to a group of people, but I can't tell you off the top of my head who exactly… and we absolutely have done Privacy Impact Assessments. I'm sure of it – I had a bunch of meetings where we discussed the impact various projects would have on privacy and I gave the business advice on what to do about that. I mean, I'm sure they took the advice, but I didn't write down what I said to them…"

When someone tells an outrageous story amongst friends, one friend usually jokes, "Pictures or it didn't happen," meaning that the person must have proof that the story occurred to be believable. A variation of this happens with data protection – proof or it didn't happen.

Demonstrating Compliance

Article 5 of GDPR expects companies to "demonstrate compliance." This means that throughout our GDPR project and forevermore, we need to keep good records of our Data Protection compliance.

We need to keep good records of the data processing we are doing under Article 30 of GDPR. This should include what we are doing with the data, who we are sharing it with and what countries it is going to. Good record keeping is critical to everything you do for Data Protection compliance. Proper corporate governance means keeping records of your thought process. If you have considered something and not made any changes because you're happy with the status quo, the fact that you considered the issue demonstrates good corporate governance.

How do I keep records so that I can demonstrate compliance?

This is a good question. There is no magic bullet or one-size-fits-all template. One way to do it is to simply get into the habit of storing items securely in a folder on your computer marked "Data Protection Compliance Records."

You should record as much as possible about what you have done in order to stay GDPR and data protection compliant.

Examples of records you should keep include:

- PIA forms you receive
- Data breaches you have logged, along with remedial advice
- Data protection policies
- Customer notices, along with any amendments you have made
- Details of training sessions you carried out
- Details and records relating to online training sessions you carried out
- Records of customer consents
- Records of the data processing you are doing
- Copies of registrations or communications with Regulators/Data Protection authorities

Make sure your compliance team knows where the folder is and allow them to add their own records to it where appropriate.

Careless & Co.

Roger Ballentine was very proud of the program he created. He had reason to be proud. By following all ten steps to GDPR compliance, he's put Careless & Co. in a great position to keep customer details safe and to protect the company from investigations and potential fines. Roger keeps a file in his computer called "Data Protection Compliance Records." In it he has:

- Three PIA forms, including the one about the CCTV project that is now closed, and two others that he was still working on.
- A record pertaining to the data breach (virus attack), along with copies of the notifications he made to the affected customers and the Data Protection Authority.
- A copy of all of Careless & Co.'s data protection policies.
- Details of the training sessions Roger carried out.
- Records of customer consents to share information with third parties.

As Roger plans for next year's initiatives, he continues to document his thought process in choosing what to focus on next.

Now It's Your Turn

What should you include in your Data Protection Compliance Records? Check the box next to each type that you have, and add additional records as needed:

- __ PIA forms you receive.
- __ Data breaches that you have logged along with remedial advice.
- __ Data Protection Policies.
- __ Customer notifications, along with any amendments you have made.
- __ Details of in-person training sessions you carried out.
- __ Details and records of online training carried out.
- __ Records of customer consents.
- __ Copies of registrations or communications with Regulators / Data Protection Authorities
- _____
- _____

- _____
- _____
- _____
- _____
- _____
- _____
- _____

The benefits of recording

GDPR introduces a higher level of data protection compliance. This will mean more regulatory action and customer complaints under GDPR.

For example, say a customer receives a marketing email that he is very unhappy about and complains to the Regulator. When the Regulator comes to your door, she is much more likely to be pacified if you have evidence to prove the customer clearly agreed to the receipt of such emails.

Keep evidence that you have carried out a change and log it with the records

A key part of demonstrating compliance is keeping evidence of the activities you perform. Let's say you trained ten people from the marketing team in London on Friday. To prove you did this, you don't just want to enter the names into an Excel sheet. You shouldn't rely on your "say so" that the training took place; you want to record evidence that the training took place.

How do you do this? Perhaps you could keep the slides you used to present the training. You may also save the email confirmation from the team leader about the session, and the note of appreciation sent to you to you thanking you for the session.

Let's say you have changed your online customer consent form. You can save the old consent form and the new consent form to show the Regulator the vital work you have carried out on this issue.

What about the GDPR project?

You should keep records of the changes you made to comply with GDPR, ideally as you go. A great way to do this is with the GDPR Implementation Table.

GDPR Implementation Table: The work carried out as part of our implementation project.

Issue	Goal	What we have done so far as of (enter date)	Outstanding	Deadline
Customer notices	Ensure all customer notices online and in paper forms are GDPR compliant	Online forms amended on 7th July 2017. See folder X for changes carried out.	Paper forms require amending	Q2 next year

Issue	Goal	What we have done so far as of (enter date)	Outstanding	Deadline
Staff training	Ensure all staff receive GDPR basic online training and deliver further specific training as required. Face-to-face training to HR, Marketing and Finance.	All online GDPR training rolled out on by end of Q3 – see folder T. HR training completed. See folder P for slides and confirmation emails.	Marketing and Finance training to be delivered Mar next year.	By year end

Careless & Co.

While Careless & Co. has come a long way toward GDPR compliance, there are still steps that must be accomplished. Roger has set out these steps in his GDPR Implementation Table. It reads:

Issue	Goal	What we have done so far as of (enter date)	Outstanding	Deadline
Customer consents	Ensure all customer consent wording online and in paper forms are GDPR compliant	Amended the online form and our paper form to comply with GDPR	None	Complete
Staff training	Ensure all staff receive training on GDPR and give specialty training to Legal, Compliance and Information Technology	Everyone has received the general training	Legal, Compliance and Information Technology specialty training is scheduled for next month	Next month

Issue	Goal	What we have done so far as of (enter date)	Outstanding	Deadline
Data Transfer	Put in place model clauses with the Australia operations	None	Complete model clause drafting and send to designated person in the Australia operation	ASAP
Data Audit and Mapping	Update the data audit and data map on an annual basis	Completed data audit and mapping for this year	Prepare emails, questionnaire and interviewee list for next year	Next spring

Now It's Your Turn

Fill in the GDPR Implementation Table for your company:

Issue	Goal	What we have done so far as of (enter date)	Outstanding	Deadline
1. **Customer consents**				
2. **Staff training**				
3. **Data Transfer**				
4. **Data Audit and Mapping**				
5.				
6.				

Issue	Goal	What we have done so far as of (enter date)	Outstanding	Deadline
7.				
8.				
9.				
10.				
11.				
12.				
13.				
14.				
15.				

Key Points:

- Proper records of our compliance must be kept under GDPR.
- Records can help vindicate the company or mitigate our position with Regulators.
- Keep records of all your data protection compliance including PIAs, Policies, Consents, and how you are processing the data.
- Keep records of all the changes you have made during your GDPR implementation project.

Notes on Implementation

_____

_____

_____

_____

_____

_____

_____

_____

_____

_____

_____

_____

_____

_____

_____

_____

_____

_____

Putting it All Together

CONGRATULATIONS ON REACHING THE end of the book! As I said in the beginning, while there are ten simple steps to GDPR implementation, the execution of these steps can be difficult and treacherous. Data privacy can be complex, convoluted and intimidating. If it is managed properly it can also benefit your customers, grow your business and help your career.

Let's revisit the key points from the book:

Step 1: Appointing Royalty: The Data Protection Officer

- Some companies are legally obligated under GDPR to appoint a DPO.
- A DPO must operate independently and report to the highest level of the company.
- You must tell Regulators and customers who your DPO is.
- Appointing a DPO may help save your company money.

Step 2: Complete the Data Audit – Otherwise Known As – Where Is All Your Data?

- Audit needed – You need to carry out a Data Audit to better understand what your company is doing with its data and what GDPR risks are present.
- Questionnaire – You should prepare a questionnaire that asks for details on how data is processed.
- Send it out – The questionnaire should be sent to all departments of the company that carry out data processing.
- Follow up with meetings – When you receive the completed questionnaires you should review them and follow up with in-person meetings to ensure you properly understand how data is processed.

Step 3: Make Your Data Map

- Prepare a data audit report – When the data audit is complete, you should prepare a report about how data is processed within your company.
- Map the data flows – Drawing a map of the data flows will help you pinpoint the issues.
- Prepare a risk register – You should prepare a risk register that outlines:
  - The major risks inherent in the way data is being used
  - How these activities could breach GDPR
  - What you need to do next.

Step 4: Get Straight on Security

- Data security is the most important part of GDPR compliance.
- Inspect your ship.
- Train your staff.
- Make sure you have adequate cybersecurity.
- Put a Data Breach Response Plan in place.
- Get cyber insured.

Step 5: Tell it like it is with Privacy Notices

- Some matters are required within Privacy Notices under GDPR (such as the contact details of the company and the DPO);
- You do not need to include every detail in the privacy notice;
- Layered is good;
- Keep it short and clear, avoid jargon, present it well, and use an appropriate tone.

Step 6: Get it in Writing: Staff Policies

- Most companies will need to change some policies to align with GDPR.
- You may need some new Data Protection Policies such as Data Breach Incident Plan, Big Data Policy, Human Resources and Data Protection Policy, Marketing and Data Protection Policy, Social Media Policy, and Bring Your Own Device Policy.
- Make sure your policies are:
  - Easy to find
  - Easy to understand
  - Short
  - Consistent
  - Enforced.

Step 7: Get on the Training Train

- Deliver basic data protection training that includes GDPR to all staff.
- Work out who needs face-to-face training.
- Make it engaging!
- Record all training you carry out.

Step 8: Assessing the Impact with PIAs

- PIAs are a fundamental part of GDPR, and it is a breach of GDPR not to use them for "high risk" data projects.
- PIAs should cover risks, recommendations, solutions, and sign off.
- Keep PIAs concise, and explain the document to your company.
- Have a PIA tracker to stay on top of your PIAs.
- Keep an eye on the projects.
- Be careful if the business wants to proceed despite having been told of serious risks.

Step 9: What to do if it all Goes Wrong – Data Breach Reporting

- Under GDPR, you have to notify the Regulator within 72 hours of a breach where it is likely to result in "a risk to the rights and freedoms of individuals."
- You must promptly notify customers about a data breach that results in a "high risk to their rights and freedoms."
- Make sure employees who learn of a Data Breach tell you about it immediately. This should be in your Data Protection Policy.
- Bad things happen sometimes – create a Data Breach Plan to guide your company in its response.

Step 10: Dealing with Third-Party Pain

- Suppliers often cause data breaches.
- GDPR expects you to choose suppliers wisely.
- Make sure your contracts contain all required GDPR clauses.
- If you are a Processor providing a service for a Controller, you have more risks now than you did before.
- Be careful with cloud providers and outsourced IT.

Record! Record! Record!

- Proper records of our compliance and processing must be kept under GDPR.
- Records can help vindicate the company or mitigate our position with Regulators.
- Keep records of all your data protection compliance including PIAs, policies, consents, and changes to your processes.
- Keep records of all the changes you have made during your GDPR implementation project.

Notes on Implementation

Notes on Implementation

Notes on Implementation

Notes on Implementation

_____

_____

_____

_____

_____

_____

_____

_____

_____

_____

_____

_____

_____

_____

_____

_____

_____

Notes on Implementation

Notes on Implementation

_____

_____

_____

_____

_____

_____

_____

_____

_____

_____

_____

_____

_____

_____

_____

_____

_____

Index

Article 15, 5
Article 17, 5
Article 20, 4
Article 28, 102, 103, 104, 105
Article 3, 3
Article 33, 5, 87, 91, 93
Article 35, 6, 77
Article 37, 5, 11, 12
Article 38, 13
Article 4, 3, 6, 101
Article 5, 6, 37, 50, 61, 78, 82, 107
Article 83, 4
Big Data, 18, 62, 63, 64, 66, 71, 78, 116
Cloud, 55, 80, 103
Consent, 7, 19
Contracts, 102
Controller, 3, 4, 5, 8, 11, 91, 93, 101, 103, 104, 105, 117
Cyber Insurance, 47, 103, 104
Cybersecurity, 47, 48
Data Audit, i, 8, 11, 17, 18, 19, 20, 26, 29, 30, 33, 35, 38, 52, 69, 111, 115
Data Breach, 5, 8, 48, 62, 63, 64, 66, 73, 87, 91, 92, 93, 95, 98, 116, 117

Data Map, i, 8, 29, 33, 52, 69, 116
Data Security, 30, 37, 38, 39, 40, 41, 42, 43, 44, 45, 48, 102
DPO, 11, 12, 13, 14, 15, 20, 39, 40, 41, 44, 45, 47, 51, 52, 58, 73, 77, 79, 80, 82, 83, 91, 92, 93, 94, 96, 115, 116
Due Diligence, 102
Employees, 5, 39, 40, 41, 44, 45, 58, 61
Indemnity, 103
PIA, 6, 77, 78, 79, 80, 81, 82, 83, 84, 107, 108, 117
Policies, 5, 6, 19, 22, 24, 39, 40, 41, 44, 45, 47, 58, 61, 62, 63, 66, 69, 70, 73, 102, 108, 116, 117
Privacy Notice, 31, 34, 50, 51, 52, 53, 54, 55, 56, 57, 58, 69
Privacy Policy, 52, 55
Processor, 3, 4, 5, 8, 11, 12, 93, 101, 102, 103, 104, 105, 117
Rapid Response Team, 63, 88, 89
Regulator, 3, 5, 6, 12, 48, 51, 75, 78, 87, 91, 92, 93, 96, 98, 103, 104, 105, 107, 109, 117
Risk Register, 32, 33, 35
Training, i, 8, 47, 69, 70, 71, 72, 73, 74, 107, 116

ABOUT THE AUTHOR

Patrick O'Kane is a lawyer and Data Protection Officer for a US Fortune 500 company. He helped lead a major GDPR implementation project across a group of 30 companies. He has written on Data Privacy for a number of publications. He lives in London.

Notes

[1] INTERNET GROWTH STATISTICS, Internet World Stats (Oct. 20, 2017), http://www.internetworldstats.com/emarketing.htm.

[2] Josh Halliday, Guardian Activate Live Coverage 2010, The Guardian (July 1, 2010), https://www.theguardian.com/media/pda/2010/jun/30/guardian-activate-summit-2010-liveblog.

[3] Gerry Smith, Massive Target Hack Traced Back to Phishing Email, Huffington Post (Feb. 12, 2014), www.huffingtonpost.com/2014/01/12/target-hack_n_4775640.html.

[4] Sruthi Ramakrishnan and Nandita Bose, Target in $18.5 million multi-state settlement over data breach, Reuters (May 23, 2017), www.reuters.com/article/us-target-cyber-settelment-idUSKBN18J2GH.

[5] TalkTalk fined £400,000 for theft of customer details, BBC News (Oct. 5, 2016), www.bbc.co.uk/news/business-37565367.

[6] Robert S. Mueller III, Director Federal Bureau of Investigation, Remarks at the RSA Cyber Security Conference (Mar. 1, 2012), https://archives.fbi.gov/archives/news/speeches/combating-threats-in-the-cyber-world-outsmarting-terrorists-hackers-and-spies.

[7] Will R. Daugherty, Human Error Is to Blame for Most Breaches, Cyber Security Trend (Jun. 6, 2016), http://www.cybersecuritytrend.com/topics/cyber-security/articles/421821-human-error-to-blame-most-breaches.htm.

[8] Special categories of data include data about race, political opinions, religion, trade union membership, genetic data, health data, or data about one's sex life or sexual orientation.

9 780993 478857